Sapori Di Calabria

By

Emilia Fusco

authorHOUSE™

1663 Liberty Drive, Suite 200
Bloomington, Indiana 47403
(800) 839-8640
www.AuthorHouse.com

First published by AuthorHouse 01/31/05

ISBN: 1-4208-0446-4 (e)
ISBN: 1-4208-0445-6 (sc)
ISBN: 1-4208-0444-8 (hc)

Library of Congress Control Number: 2004098564

Printed in the United States of America
Bloomington, Indiana

This book is printed on acid-free paper.

TABLE OF CONTENTS

A TE MAMMA VOGLIO DEDICARE QUEST LIBRO

To my Mother

Mamma! You have given our family so much love and understanding. You have supported us and given us your unconditional love during times of stress, pain and heartbreak. You were a Mamma that was always more than willing to add that loving touch that makes life more fulfilling.

I miss you Mamma!

You overcame all obstacles in your life and made the best of each situation, thinking not for yourself but for your family.

Even when your family, on occasion, overlooked or took you for granted, you still continued to serve, love, and care for and teach us. I never forget all the things I learned from you. You taught me everything I know; how to sew, embroider and some of the most important things I learned while I was with you in the kitchen. You were the best Mamma!

I pray to God that you know how much I love you and miss you in our lives. You are always on my mind and in my heart, and when I lost you, I lost a part of myself. I did not just lose my Mamma, but I lost my best friend. I hope you know I always love you Mamma!

A day does not go by that I don't think of you, and I always miss you Mamma.

I miss my Papa and brother Salvatore. You are all there together near God.

Mamma! I want you to know that in my eyes, heart and mind without reservation, you still are and always will be the best Mamma and best friend any daughter could hope for. With no doubt in my mind and in my heart you are "FOREVER MOTHER OF THE YEAR "

Love Always,

Your daughter, Emilia.

GRAZIE ALLA MIA FAMIGLIA

Thank You to My Family

To Peter my husband, for his love, understanding and for supporting me no matter what.

To my son Alberto and my daughter-in-law Kristine for being the beautiful family they are and for giving Peter and I two beautiful granddaughters, Cara Mia and Gianna Maria. (Cara Mia is my helper in the kitchen.)

To my daughter Silvia and my son-in-law Shawn for being a beautiful family and giving Peter and I a beautiful grandson, Anthony Michael.

Papa and I feel so blessed and are so proud of you. We love you all very much.

To my mother-in-law Nancy for always being there for us. Thank you Mom.

To my niece Maria Concetta Russo for providing me with the pictures of our town and of Calabria.

To Mr. Aurelio Tuccio for providing me with the crivi story.

And I would to thank you God for having blessed me with a loving family and for being with me during my moments of need. I couldn't have done this book without the love from my family and God in my heart.

Thank You,

Emilia

LA STORIA DAI CRIVI E CRIVARI DI MONTEPAONE

This is the story of the baskets from my home town, Montepaone.

What are "crivi"?

They are beautiful baskets made in my home town and is a family business. The husband, wife, and sometime the children, work together. The baskets are use to sift corn and wheat and are made in small, medium and large sizes of both oval and round shapes. There are also "double trim" baskets that are used especially as fruit baskets at the center of the kitchen table, and the fruit basket you see on this page is a double trim basket.

The materials used are called jungos, vrudo, and surko, ziparu, and strosa. All of these materials are picked by the town farmers.

In 1955 there were 150 professional crivi makers. In the 1980's there were about 25. Today there are only 3 remaining.

We used to roll our gnocchi on the crivi, which gave them a beautiful shape. We do not use a fork to shape the gnocchi like they do in northern Italy.

I want to thank you Mr. Aurelio Tuccio for sending me the crivi story. Mr. Tuccio lives in our home town, Montepaone in Provincia Catanzaro, and he is an architect.

I WOULD LIKE TO INTRODUCE YOU TO MY HOMETOWN: MONTEPAONE.

With a population of 4,406, Montepaone is a provincia in Catanzaro. Its territory rises from the sea to an altitude of about 367 meters and covers an area close to 17 km. Montepaone Lido, its beach, is 3.5 km, and the town is 32 km from Catanzaro Provincia.

The old costumes are colorful and very traditional. The photo you see is my beautiful daughter Silvia. She was 5 years old when this picture was taken. She participated in Carnival party with about 500 other people, and everyone one wore the costumes from their place of origin in Italy. My daughter Silvia wears the beautiful costume from my home town.

Not to bad for a little Calabrisella!

The organic farming production in Calabria is healthy and free from chemicals.

The Calabrian population is a great consumer of these resources: homemade bread, cheese, olives, fresh fruit and vegetables. We preserve tomatoes, tomato sauce, beans, asparagus, artichokes, peppers and fruit to last through the whole year.

From our fresh lemons, we make our homemade liquor (Limoncello): and citron, liqueurs, and (Nocino) from walnuts skin, this type of liqueurs, is brown in color, and strongly aromatic. At Christmas it is traditional to make zeppoli, "fry dough", mostacciole, susimelli and cecerata. Cecerata is a pastry made with small eggs pasta.

The culture of Calabria is also involves fishing along the shores from the city of Cosenza to Reggio Calabria. The Mediterranean is rich in tuna, anchovies, and anchovies with chili pepper, mullet, bass, and clams. The most expense fish is the neonata or bianco mangiare.

The neonata is a special fish for making soup, and be fried with a batter made of flour, water, eggs, grated cheese, and a pinch of salt and black pepper. Spoon into a hot oil and fried until golden.

Sheep, goats and pigs are very important to the farmers in Calabria. The goats mostly provide milk for many special Italian cheeses, mozzarella the buffalo, casciocavallo, casciotte, fresh and dry ricotta cheese and pecorino (Romano) cheese.

The people of Calabria also make beautiful handicrafts and artwork. Wood work, ceramic, gold jewels, stone, copper and wrought iron. There is fabric made with beautiful designs and embroidery.

All of this tradition from Calabria is handed down from one generation to the other, as I have passed all of this to my children and grandchildren.

The 2 photos are of my town Montepaone and of the marine at Montepaone Lido.

CALABRIA AND ITS 5 DISTRICTS

The district of Catanzaro: develops round one of the most interesting geographic place of the whole Italian peninsula: here only 35 kilometric divide the Jonio Sea form the Tirreno Sea. From the mountains that face the isthmus, it easy compare the blue of the two sea and enjoy dawns the sunsets in with the sun rises and finishes one's daily course from the waters of the sea rich of history.

The district of Cosenza: is quite property. Is considered the most interesting cultural and historical destinations. Paola is the synthesis of the great religiousness of the Calabria people; here there is the (S. Franceso di Paola Sanctuary, patron Saint of Calabria and of sea folk.

The young district of Vibo Valente: has two centres, the hilly and the sea district with the respective port from with leave the summer connection with the Eolie Isles.

The district of Crotone: offers occasions of historical reflections and of landscapes that brings us the splendor of the Magna Grecian. From one Kilometric form Crotone is Capo Colonna, one the most diffuse symbol of the Calabria.

The big district of Reggio Calabria keeps in one of the most well known National museum. The district is rich in anthropology elements with unite in harmony the natural landscapes, and place of history. Form here Messina; first City of Sicily looks like to touch oneself with the hands when the effect.

Calabria peninsula is narrow approximately 250 Fm. long. In all 5 districts are 402 Cities and Towns. There is more to be discovered the beauty of Southern of Italy, perhaps we can share more at another time.

Thank you for spending time with me, and learning about my heritage and the beauty of Calabria.

Emilia Fusco.

INTRODUCTION
GUIDLINES FOR A HEALTHY DIET

EAT LESS SATURATED FAT:

Saturated fat raises blood cholesterol more than anything else in the diet. It is a type of fat found in large quantities in animal products. The key is to eat much less saturated fat.

The major food sources for saturated fat are cheeses, butter, fatty meat, cold cuts, poultry skin, whole milk, shortening, chocolate and coconut.

Steaming, broiling and roasting are methods of cooking that do not add fat to a meal. Add herbs and spice to flavor your meals instead of oil or butter. Marinating meat, fish in wine, soy sauce, herbs and spices. When baking use wine or lemon juice rather then oil or butter.

EAT LESS CHOLESTEROL:

The body naturally produces cholesterol. Dietary cholesterol is also found in foods of animal origin, but not in plants. This dietary cholesterol tends to raise blood cholesterol. Major food sources: eggs, organic meats, shellfish, shrimp, crab, squid, dairy products, poultry and fish.

When baking use wine or lemon juice rather then oil or butter. This will help save you from loading your meals with sodium and cholesterol.

EAT LESS TRANS-FATTY ACIDS:

Trans-fatty acids are produced during the processing of margarines and vegetable oils. Any processed foods made with partially hydrogenated oil contains trans-fatty acidy. Trans-fatty acids also raise cholesterol levels. Major food sources are margarines, vegetable shortenings and store bought cookies and crackers.

Pastries, deep-fried food such as doughnuts French fries, and fast food, use MONOUNSATURATED FATS: When substituted for saturated fat, monounsaturated fats can help reduce your blood cholesterol. Such unsaturated fats are found in greatest amounts in food from plants. Major food sources are olive oil, canola oil, peanut oil nuts, avocado, pickled herring and peanut butter.

EAT MORE FIBER:

Eating foods high in soluble fiber may help reduce your cholesterol levels. Major food sources: oatmeal, oat bran, apples, prunes, broccoli, brussel sprouts, carrots, corn, yams, kidney beans and black-eyed peas.

EAT MORE FRUITS AND VEGETABLES

Populations that consume higher amounts of fruits and vegetables, have lower rates of heart disease and stroke.

The U.S. department of Agriculture's new Food Pyramid recommends 2-4 servings of fruit and 3-5 servings of vegetables each day.

GENERAL GUIDELINES ABOUT RESTAURANTS:

Always ask about the menu to find out if they cook without butter and oil. Many Italian restaurants include special low fat dishes, where meats and vegetables are broiled, baked, roasted, steamed or grilled. Ask about the fat they do use. For very light dishes, extra-virgin olive oil is the best. Avoid fried food, pastry, tiramisu, pasta carbonara, stuffed shells, antipasti, cheese, and sauce bascianella.

FOODS TO CHOOSE:

Vegetable and minestrone soups, steamed fish and pasta with salsa primavera with assorted vegetables in the sauce. Eat chicken cacciatore, roasted or baked turkey, veal scaloppini or veal piccante, and fish. Eat your salad before your main dish, also, be sure to trim all of the visible fat.

When you make a soup make a day before you need it, put it in the refrigerator overnight (after it has cooled some) and before you reheat the soup, skim off any fat that has risen to the top with a spatula. You really can cut the calories per serving in half.

Blend half the vegetables in the soup and mix them back in with rest with the soup. This gives it a rich taste and texture.

Beans, or fagioli in Italian, are definitely part of a healthy diet, as beans are fat free, rich in protein, iron, potassium and fiber. Beans help lower cholesterol and help thin blood sugar levels. Beans can be used as first or second dishes, to make pasta and beans, minestrone soups, and over bruschetta with roasted peppers. There are so many names in Italy for different types of beans: cannellini, roman, burlotta, five beans, ceci, red beans, green beans, and more.

Dry beans need to be soaked for 6 hours or over night. When you soak beans, use 1 part beans to 5 parts water and when boiling use 1 pound of beans per 8 cups of water.

MAINTAIN A DESIRABLE BODY WEIGHT:

You can achieve this with proper food choices and daily exercise. Weight can be reached and maintained by taking the correct steps. This helps keep your heart in shape! You may ask yourself, what can I do to change my eating habits to keep my heart healthy?" The types of food you eat can help lower your "bad" cholesterol level. By reducing these levels, you can decrease your risk of developing further heart disease.

LABEL CLAIM DEFINITIONS

"FREE" (meaning "without" or "zero"): foods which contain not a trivial amount of a particular nutrient. Furthermore, calorie-free means fewer than 5 calories per serving and fat-free means less then 0.5 gm fat par serving.

Note: pay attention to this, in this book you read a large expansion on the Italia cuisine: plenty of vegetable dish, salad and past dishes. In Italy soup is served as primo dish (first course or before the pasta.)

You can make a whole meal with soups, by adding beans, potatoes, arugula or escarole, carrots, and you have minestrone. Minestrone always improves when cooked and reheated as leftovers, served with crostini or bruschetta. When you make a salad, you can be prepare it in advance to save time, but never mix the salad until it is needed, or the lettuce will become soggy and brown.

There are so many meals you can make in 30 minutes or less. For combination dishes such as sandwiches, salads, casseroles, pizza and other mixed dishes, look up the calorie value for each ingredient of food in the dish. Then add them up for a total.

Do you love the olive oil, sausage, pasta, lasagnas, and all the good cakes? You can cut the calories and fat consumed by cutting the portion you eat in half. Some people think the ultimate Italian meals are loaded with a large amount of butter, fats, oils and cheeses. This is not true. You can enjoy Italian food and cut out the fat, but still enjoy the taste by using herbs and plenty of spices. You can create new flavors and good taste combinations, without loading your dishes with fat, sodium and cholesterol.

TIPS TO SAVE YOU TIME IN THE KITCHEN

When you have time to spare, use it to chop vegetables that you use frequently, such as onions and garlic. Place small amounts in freezer bags for use later. You can do this the same way with all vegetables; just put all vegetables into separate bags or in plastic containers. Make sure to label all of the bags with name and date before you put them into the freezer!

You can also save time by cutting all the vegetables the day before or washing and cutting meats. Just dry and refrigerate them overnight or for the next day. When going to the supermarket you can also by all vegetables chopped from the salad bar, and this can save you even more time.

Add finishing touches to the dish: Decorate with fresh herbs, such fresh basil, fresh chopped parsley, mint, fresh scallions and grated cheese.

When going to the supermarket, try to by everything you need that day. It is easier to going to the kitchen pantry and not to the supermarket.

Always try to make less time in the kitchen and more time for yourself and guests when they arrive to your home.

When buying lemons, each will make 2 tablespoons of lemon zest. You can do this ahead just like the vegetables and use when needed.

When you need to crush chili peppers: Use a pair of gloves, or put peppers into sealed plastic bag and crush with a rolling pin. You can also simply put the peppers into a blender.

I hope that these tips will save you time in the kitchen and give you more time to enjoy with your guests.

<Have fun! Life is beautiful in the kitchen. Emilia>

1. STARTERS, APPETIZERS AND SNACKS

COLAZIONE DI VEGETALE E FRUTTA

Fruit Breakfast

INGREDIENTS

3 cups chopped fresh pineapple

1 ½ cups fresh raspberries

1½ cups low-fat vanilla yogurt

1½ medium firm banana, peeled and sliced

1 cup chopped dates

½ cup sliced almonds, toasted

DIRECTIONS

In 6 glasses, layer evenly: pineapple, raspberries, yogurt, banana, and dates. Sprinkle the top with almonds.

Remember! Breakfast is a very important part of your daily meals.

<Enjoy! Emilia>

EMILIA'S BRUSCHETTA

Emilia's Bruschetta

INGREDIENTS

6 recipes of roasted red peppers

1 can (15½ oz) cannellini beans

12 slices Italian bread

½ cup marinara sauce

DIRECTIONS

Preheat oven at 375 F.

Toast bread slices until golden, approximately 1 minute.

Rinse cannellini beans and transfer to a small bowl; add marinara sauce, gently toss, put the bowl in the microwave and heat for 2 minutes.

Prepare roasted red peppers according to the recipe. Cut lengthwise and half inch wider.

Lay half of sliced peppers over the toasted Italian bread and add 2 tablespoons cannellini beans. Serve when bruschetta is hot.

Makes 12 servings.

<Have fun! Emilia>

RICOTTA BRUSCHETTA

Ricotta Bruschetta

INGREDIENTS

1 cup ricotta cheese

1 teaspoon sage, chopped

1 teaspoon fresh basil leaves, chopped

½ teaspoon fresh ground white pepper

1 tablespoon extra virgin olive oil

DIRECTIONS

In a small bowl combine all the ingredients from recipe mix with fork to blend all the spices together. To serve, slice loaf of French bread, ½ inch thick. Put slices into a toaster, toast to a golden color: spread ricotta cheese over the toast.

This is also good cheese spread to put over spaghetti: Cook 1 pound of spaghetti in a large pan, and lightly salt the water according to package directions. Drain, and add 2 tablespoons hot water from the spaghetti to the ricotta mixture. Transfer spaghetti into a serving platter, mix in the ricotta mixture, toss and serve hot.

<Buon Appetito! Emilia>

BRUSCHETTA MEDITERRANEA

Mediterranean Bruschetta

INGREDIENTS

4 slice white bread

4 fresh mozzarella slices

2 tomatoes thinly sliced

1 Italian eggplant, thin sliced and roasted

4 teaspoons extra virgin olive oil

1 egg boiled and sliced

2 tablespoons fresh basil, thinly sliced

DIRECTIONS

Preheat oven to 300 F.

Cover each slice of bread with a mozzarella slice, a slice of the roasted eggplant, and a slice of egg. Toast bruschetta in oven for 2 minuets, then remove and top each slice with basil.

<If you do not want the egg, you can omit them from the recipe.>

Serve hot as antipasto or side dish.

<Buon Appetito! Emilia>

BRUSCHETTA PIZZAIOLA DI CALABRIA

Calabrian Bruschetta

INGREDIENTS

4 slice with bread toast

2 buffalo mozzarella slices

1 cup tomatoes, peeled and chopped

12 flat anchovy fillets rolled with capers in olive oil

1 tablespoon olive oil

1 teaspoon oregano fresh or flakes

1 pinch salt and pepper

DIRECTIONS

Preheat oven to 300 F.

Mix tomatoes, oregano, salt, pepper and oil. Divide the tomato 4 and cover the sliced bread with tomato, then a slice of mozzarella cheese, rollup anchovies.

Put sliced bruschetta on a rack let bake in the oven for 2 minutes until mozzarella melts over the tomato.

Serve as a lunch or a snack.

<Have a good time with your friends and family. Emilia>

CALAMARI FRITTI

Fried Squid

INGREDIENTS

2 pound calamari

2 cups vegetable oil

1 teaspoon salt

½ teaspoon ground black pepper

1 cup skim milk

½ cup corn flour

DIRECTIONS

Wash, clean and cut calamari into rings. (If this is too much for you, the supermarket or your fish store can clean it for you.)

Mix last 4 ingredients well, and then dip squid into the batter.

Heat oil, add squib and fry until golden. When they are golden, drain with a spatula and put into a dish with paper towels to remove excess oil.

Serve with sliced lemon or dip into a puttanesca sauce for antipasto.

To clean calamari: All you need is a good knife with a strong handle. First you must cut tentacles from the head below the eyes. Pull out the cartilage and insides. Wash under cool water, clean the skin and cut into small pieces or leave whole and stuff.

<Have fun! Emilia>

FUNGHI RIPIENI

Stuffed Mushrooms

INGREDIENTS

21 medium mushrooms

¼ cup lemon juice

4 oz. Italian sausage

3 cloves of garlic, peeled and chopped

½ cup seasoned Italian breadcrumbs

1 tablespoon Italian parsley, chopped

¼ teaspoon black pepper

DIRECTIONS

Preheat oven to 375 F.

Remove mushroom stems and mince them. Brush mushroom caps with lemon juice to prevent discoloration. Remove the Italian sausage from its casing and place in a bowl. Add chopped stems, garlic, salt, pepper, breadcrumbs, and chopped parsley and mix well.

Spoon stuffing into mushrooms on lightly greased baking dish for 20 minutes or until sausage is no longer pink.

Makes 7 servings.

<Have fun! Emilia>

ANTIPASTO (INSALATA CAPRESE)

Fresh Mozzarella & Tomato Appetizer

INGREDIENTS

12 large buffalo mozzarella, sliced ½ inch thick

12 tomatoes, sliced ½ inch thick

12 fresh basil leaves

2 tablespoons balsamic vinegar

¼ cup extra virgin olive oil

¼ teaspoon dried oregano flakes

¼ teaspoon black pepper

¼ teaspoon salt

DIRECTIONS

Lay the tomatoes flat in large serving dish. Top each slice of tomato with 1 fresh basil leaf. Top with sliced mozzarella cheese.

Mix balsamic vinegar, oil, oregano, salt and pepper. Mix well and sprinkle over tomato mozzarella stacks.

Makes 6 servings

<Double or triple quantities of the recipe for large party. Emilia>

ANTIPASTO DI MOZZARELLA

Mozzarella Appetizer

INGREDIENTS

12 slice fresh mozzarella, bocconcine

½ cup fresh basil, chopped

½ cup sun-dried tomatoes packed in olive oil, chopped

DIRECTIONS

Slice mozzarella ½ inch thick. Top with a leaf of fresh basil and a sun-dried tomato.

Serve on a lettuce leaf and sprinkle with the oil that the tomatoes were packed in. Prepare 2 for each person to serve as an appetizer.

Makes 6 servings

<Double the amount of the recipe if you having a party. Emilia.>

PANZARELLE FOR ANTIPASTO

Baked Appetizer

INGREDIENTS

1 large long potato

1 cup flour

½ teaspoon baking powder

1 egg, beaten

½ teaspoon salt

2 oz. melted butter

4 oz. prosciutto, sliced thick

4 oz. fontina cheese, thinly sliced

DIRECTIONS

Preheat oven to 350 F.

Peel and mash potato with a fork or rice mill.

In a bowl mix flour, baking powder, the egg, potato, salt and butter. Mix well and cover and with a dishtowel for 10 minutes.

Sprinkle flour on a wooden surface and roll the dough into a very thin, flat square.

Cut dough into four 3 inch squares and add Prosciutto pieces and cheese. Brush around the edges with water, and then take one corner and fold it over to the other corner to make a triangle.

Seal the edges with a fork and make a small slit in the top. Brush the top with beaten egg. Bake on a greased pan in preheated oven for 10 minutes or until golden.

<Enjoy! Emilia>

MOZZARELLA ANTIPASTO CON IL PEPERONCINO

Mozzarella With A Twist

INGREDIENTS

2 pounds mozzarella cheese

3 tablespoons pesto sauce

1 teaspoon crushed red pepper

2 tablespoons fresh basil leaves, chopped

DIRECTIONS

Cube mozzarella and toss with pesto sauce, sprinkle with crushed red pepper and decorate with a sprinkle of fresh basil leaves.

This makes a perfect center for a cheese platter.

Makes 20 servings.

<Have fun! Emilia>

POLPETTE DI CARNE

Meatballs

INGREDIENTS

1 pound ground beef

1 pound ground pork

½ cup Romano cheese, grated

2 tablespoons parsley, chopped

1 pinch ground black pepper

1 cup breadcrumbs

1 slice Italian bread

2 eggs

1 clove garlic, peeled and chopped

1 cup vegetable oil

DIRECTIONS

In a bowl mix all the ingredients well: Shape mixture into 1-½ inch diameter balls and set on a plate. Heat vegetable oil in a non-stick skillet, and when the oil is hot add meatballs and fry in batches of 2 (or more) until golden brown.

You can also bake the meatballs. Cover a baking sheet with parchment paper and bake in a preheated 375 f. oven for 15 minutes or until light brown.

Meanwhile, make 1 recipe of marinara sauce. Add meatballs to the marinara sauce and cook for 45 minutes to 1 hour. Serve with cooked pasta of your choice, on sandwiches or even over a slice of pizza.

<Buon Appetito! Emilia>

POLPETTE SEMPLICE CON POCO CALORIE

Low Calorie Meatball

INGREDIENTS

1 pound ground veal

1 pound turkey

1 large egg

2 eggs whites

1 cup seasoned breadcrumbs

¼ cup Parmesan cheese, grated

¼ teaspoon ground black pepper

2 tablespoons marinara sauce

1 cup vegetable oil for frying

DIRECTIONS

In a large mix bowl mix ground veal and turkey, egg whites and whole egg, and then thoroughly mix in all the rest of the ingredients except the oil.

Using your hand or a small ice scream scoop, make the meatballs about one and a half inches round.

In a large skillet, heat oil and fry the meatballs until brown on all sides.

Transfer each meatball to a dish covered with paper towels to drain the excess.

This recipe can be doubled for a large party. It can also been made days in advance before you need them. Meatballs can go straight from the freezer to the sauce. This will save you time to spend with your family and guests.

<Buon Appetito! Emilia>

PROSCIUTTO COTTO ROTOLATO

Ham & Cheese Rollups

INGREDIENTS

½ pound cream cheese

¼ pound Genoa salami sliced

1 tablespoon horseradish

½ pound ham, sliced

DIRECTIONS

In food processor, use steel blade to combine cream cheese, Genoa salami and horseradish. Spread each slice of ham with 2 tablespoons of cream cheese mixture, then roll the ham lengthwise and cut into 8 bite size pieces.

Serve on platter decorated with carved vegetables.

Makes 60 hors d'oeuvres.

<Have great time. Emilia>

BASTONCINI DI ASPARICI PER LA FESTA

Rolled Up Asparagus for Your Party

INGREDIENTS

24 asparagus spears, trimmed to 6 inches

4 sheets of store bought pastry dough

12 slices of prosciutto

1 package (8 oz.) cream cheese, softened

½ cup Parmesan cheese, grated

¼ teaspoon fresh ground black pepper

1 egg, beaten

DIRECTIONS

Preheat oven to 375 F.

Wash and dry asparagus and then trim them to 6 inch long.

Flatten pastry dough with rolling pin and divide each sheet into 6 equal portions.

In a small bowl mix cream cheese, grated Parmesan cheese, salt and ground black pepper. Spoon cheese mixture over the piece of pastry dough, and then add 1 slice of prosciutto and one asparagus spear on each.

Roll pastry dough and place seam down on a non-stick baking sheet. Brush rolled up pastry with egg. Bake in preheated oven for 10 minutes or until golden and lightly brown.

Makes 24 Serving.

<A nice presentation for a brunch. Enjoy! Emilia>

TRADITIONAL CHEESE FONDUE

Cheese Fondue

INGREDIENTS

3 cloves of garlic, peeled and cut in half

1 pound fontina cheese, shredded

1 tablespoon lemon juice

4 tablespoons corn starch

16 oz. California white wine

1 shot Chardonnay

½ teaspoon ground white pepper

1 pinch grated nutmeg

Crusty Italian bread, cut into 1-inch cubes

You need a fondue pot with a burner and fondue forks.

DIRECTIONS

Rub fondue pot with garlic and discard garlic.

Add shredded cheese, wine and lemon juice to the pot and begin heating on stove at medium heat while stirring constantly. After cheese has melted, mix cornstarch with chardonnay in a small bowl, and then add mixture to the cheese. Stir until smooth, add pepper and nutmeg, and place over fondue burner.

Spear one cube of bread on fondue fork and dip into fondue using a figure eight motion so that you are stirring while you are dipping.

<Enjoy! Emilia>

BRODO DI PESCE

Fish Stock

INGREDIENTS

2 ½ quarts water

2 salmon or tuna heads

2 carrots, chopped

1 cup red onion, chopped

1 cup celery, chopped

4 bay leaves

3 lemons, thickly sliced

DIRECTIONS

Wash fish heads, place in a pan of boiling water, and remove any scum that forms with a draining spatula. Add all the vegetables, cover, and simmer for about 45 minutes, then strain. Keep in the refrigerator for 4 days or frozen.

The stock can be frozen up to three months, but allow the stock to cool somewhat before putting in the freezer or refrigerator.

<Have fun! Emilia>

BRODO DI VEGETALI

Vegetable Stock

INGREDIENTS

2 ½ quarts of water

1 cup carrots, chopped

1 cup celery, chopped

4 bay leaves

12 cups fresh parsley

1 cup onions, chopped

2 cloves of garlic

2 fresh leaves of sage

1 teaspoon pepper

DIRECTIONS

Bring all vegetables to a boil. Remove any scum that forms with a spatula. Cover and simmer for 45 minutes.

Strain the stock and let cool. The stock can be stored in the refrigerator for 4 days or freezer for up to 3 months.

<Enjoy! Emilia>

STRACCIATELLA

Chicken Soup with Eggs & Cheese

INGREDIENTS

6 cups chicken stock

6 eggs, separated

¾ cup Parmesan cheese, grated

3 lemon juice

DIRECTIONS

Heat chicken broth in a saucepan.

In a small bowl beat the egg yolks together with the Parmesan. Separately, beat egg whites until they look like snow. Gently mix the egg whites, lemon juice into the yolk cheese, mixture with a spatula.

When the stock comes to a boil, pour egg mixture into soup. Break the egg mixture with a big fork or use a hand whisker.

Serve hot with Italian bread sticks.

Makes 6 servings.

<Enjoy! Emilia>

ZUPPA DI LENTICCHIE

Lentil Soup

INGREDIENTS

3 cups water

1 ½ cup dried lentils

1 cup carrots, chopped ½ inch thick

1 cup grape tomatoes

½ cup celery, chopped

1 small leek, chopped

1 tablespoon extra virgin olive oil

½ onion, chopped

½ pound lean veal stew meat

2 tablespoons dry white wine

1 tablespoon cornstarch

DIRECTIONS

Rinse and sort lentils with cold water. (Remove the "bad ones". They will float to the top.) In a large saucepan bring the water to a boil and add ingredients up to and including the leeks. Bring back to a boil, and then simmer on low heat for 35 minutes.

While the lentils and vegetables are cooking, heat the oil and sauté onion until golden, then add veal and sauté until light brown.

In a small bowl dissolve cornstarch into the wine and add to the veal. Stir for one minute, and then add the veal mixture to the lentil soup. If soup is too thick, add a cup of water. Cover and let simmer for 10 minutes longer.

Serve with Italian crostini or crackers.

Makes 4 servings

<Buon Appetito! Emilia>

ZUPPA DI LENTICCHIE E PROSCIUTTO COTTO

Lentil Soup with Ham

INGREDIENTS

8 cups water

1 pound of lentils

1 cup carrots, chopped

1 cup celery, chopped

1 pound ham, cubed

1 cup onion, chopped

1 teaspoon black pepper

4 tablespoons sherry

DIRECTIONS

Wash and drain lentils, then clean and thinly slice carrots and celery. Place lentils in large pot and add all remaining ingredients except sherry. Cover and bring to boil, the reduce heat and simmer for 2 hours, stirring often.

Soup is done when lentils are soft and blended. For a thicker broth use less water. Just before serving, add sherry and stir well.

Make 6 servings.

<Buon Appetito! Emilia>

MINESATRA DI VEGETALI

Vegetable Soup

INGREDIENTS

2 cups olive oil

1 cup Italian pancetta, chopped into small cubes

2 cloves of garlic, peeled and chopped

1 cup onion, chopped

1 cup celery, chopped

¾ cup carrots, chopped

¾ cup all-purpose potatoes, peeled and cut into 1 inch cubes

4 cups cabbage, shredded

3 large tomatoes, peeled, seeded and chopped

1 cup fresh or frozen green beans

2-½ quart water

1 cup Italian zucchini, cut in half and slice ¼ inch thick

(Scoop out the insides before cutting)

¾ cup orecchiette pasta

1 cup cooked cannellini beans

1 cup pinto or Roman red beans

½ teaspoon salt

1 teaspoon ground black pepper

½ cup Parmesan cheese, grated

¼ teaspoon Italian parsley, chopped

DIRECTIONS

In a large saucepan, heat oil and sauté pancetta until crisp. With spatula take pancetta of the saucepan, sauté garlic until golden, and then add onions, celery, potatoes, cabbage, carrots and tomatoes. Sauté for 3 minutes, and then add green beans and water. Bring to a boil and then simmer partially covered for 20 minutes.

Add zucchini, orecchiette pasta, and salt and ground pepper, and add all the beans. Cook pasta until al dente, add ½ the cheese, and stir. Serve in a large bowl and sprinkle with the remaining Parmesan cheese and parsley. Serve hot with garlic bread.

<Enjoy! And Buon Appetito! Emilia>

MINESTRA DI VEGETALE

Vegetable Stew

INGREDIENTS

8 cups water

1 ½ cup celery, chopped into 1 inch pieces

1 can (15 oz.) red roman beans

1 pound fresh green beans, trimmed on each side and cut into 1 inch pieces

1 cup Italian zucchini, cut in half and sliced 1 inch thick (scoop out the insides before cutting)

½ cup green onion, chopped

1 can (15 oz.) crushed tomatoes

1-½ cup potatoes, peeled and cut into 1 inch cubes

4 beef bouillon cubes

1 teaspoon salt

½ teaspoon ground black pepper

2 cups fresh escarole, chopped

1 bell pepper green, seeded and cut into 1 inch pieces

1 bell red pepper, seeded and cut into 1 inch pieces

DIRECTIONS

In a large pot, add all the ingredients, cover and bring to a boil. Lower heat and simmer, keeping covered, for 30 minutes.

Test to see if more salt or pepper is needed. Serve hot with seasoned bread sticks.

Makes 10 cups of vegetable soup.

<Have fun! Emilia>

MINESTRA DI VEGETALE (PER 2 PRANZI)

Minestrone (1 Pot = 2 Meals)

INGREDIENTS

1 pound green beans, trimmed on each side and cut into 1 inch pieces

½ teaspoon olive oil

2 cloves of garlic, peeled and chopped

1 can (15 oz.) crushed tomatoes peeled

2 large potatoes, peeled and cut into 1 inch cube

1 cup celery, chopped

2 small zucchini, cut in half and sliced 1 1/2 inch thick

(Scoop out the insides before cutting)

2 fresh basil leaves

1 teaspoon salt

¼ teaspoon ground black pepper

2 cans (15 oz.) of cannellini or roman beans

DIRECTIONS

Steam or boil green beans until tender and set aside.

In a large saucepan, heat oil and sauté chopped garlic until golden. Add crushed tomatoes and simmer on low heat for 5 minutes. Add 4 cups of water, the potatoes, celery, zucchini, basil leaves, and salt and pepper. Cook until zucchini and potatoes are tender.

Add cannellini beans and cook for 1 minute until beans are warm. Transfer to soup bowls and sprinkle two tablespoons of Romano cheese over the soup. Serve hot.

Eat minestrone the first day and save the leftovers for the second day. While the minestrone is reheating, cook 1 cup ditalini pasta or rice, and when pasta is done, drain and add to minestrone.

I make this dish almost once every week in the winter. I benefit two times from this dish, as it is light, healthy, and it saves me time to spend with my grandchildren.

<Buon Appetito! Emilia>

MINESTRA DI FAGIOLI

Minestrone with Beans

INGREDIENTS

1 pound dry cannellini beans

¼ cup olive oil

2 tablespoons butter

½ small onion, chopped

1 tablespoon flour

1 cup heavy cream

1 teaspoon salt

½ teaspoon ground pepper

½ cup scallions, chopped

DIRECTIONS

In a big saucepan soak beans the night before, then cook according to package directions. It usually takes about 20 to 30 minutes for the beans to cook. Leave the beans in the same saucepan to keep warm.

In a large skillet, heat oil and butter, and then sauté onion until golden. Add 3 scoops of warm water from the beans and a pinch of salt. Cook on low heat for 5 minutes.

Drain beans and toss into the skillet. If you need to, add more hot water and simmer for 2 minutes. Take skillet off the stove, mix in the heavy cream and serve hot. Before serving, taste to see if you need more salt or pepper, and garnish with the chopped scallions.

Makes 6 servings.

<This is a very healthy dish. Buon Appetito! Emilia>

PASTA E FAGIOLI

Ditalini Pasta & Beans

INGREDIENTS

1 pound ditalini pasta

¼ cup olive oil

2 oz. pork guanciale or Italian pancetta, cut into ½ inch cubes

2 cloves of garlic, peeled and chopped

2 tablespoons onion, minced

2 bay leaves

1 can (16 oz.) diced tomatoes

¼ teaspoon oregano flakes

2 fresh basil leaves

1 teaspoon salt

¼ teaspoon ground black pepper

½ cup red wine

1 can (15 ½ oz.) cannellini beans

¼ cup Parmesan cheese, grated

1 tablespoon Italian parsley, chopped

DIRECTIONS

In a saucepan add 1 tablespoon oil and sauté pancetta until brown. Transfer pancetta to a dish covered with paper towels to drain the excess oil. Discard the fat from the skillet; add the remaining oil and sauté garlic and onion until golden. Add tomatoes, oregano, and black pepper, salt, and basil leaves. Cook on medium heat for 10 minutes. Add wine and pancetta and let cook for 5 minutes longer. Mix in the beans. Cover and cook until pasta is finished cooking.

Cook ditalini pasta according to the package directions. Drain some water off of the pasta and add the bean mixture. Transfer soup to a big serving bowl and add half the cheese. Mix, then add remaining cheese and chopped parsley. Serve hot.

Makes 6 servings.

<From my table to yours. Buon Appetito! Emilia>

ZUPPA DI VONGOLE

Clam Soup

INGREDIENTS

3 pounds clams

3 cups dry white wine

¼ cup olive oil

2 cloves of garlic, peeled and chopped

½ cup, minced onion

6 anchovy filets, thinly chopped

¼ cup marinara sauce

1 teaspoon salt

½ teaspoon ground black pepper

2 tablespoons Italian parsley, chopped

DIRECTIONS

Put clams in a large pot and add the white wine. Turn heat on high and cover to steam until clams open. Discard all clams that stay closed. Remove clams from the shells and discard the shells. Strain the clam stock and return it to the pot. Add clams to the pot in the hot liquid.

Heat oil in a skillet and sauté garlic and onion until golden. Drain the juice from the clams and add to the skillet. Add anchovies, marinara sauce, salt and pepper, mix well and cover. Simmer for 4 minutes until the clams blend in with sauce. Transfer soup into serving bowls and garnish with parsley. Serve with Italian bread sticks or plain bruschetta.

<Buon Appetito! Emilia>

IL RE DELLA COLAZIONE ITALIANA

Hot Italian King Sandwiches

INGREDIENTS

3 loaves French bread

10 oz. Parma prosciutto, sliced

10 oz. Italian mortadella, sliced

10 oz. hot soppressata, sliced

10 oz. provolone cheese, sliced

10 oz. Genoa salami, sliced

6 roasted red pepper slices

3 tomatoes, sliced

3 cups chopped green salad, for top the sandwiches

6 tablespoons extra virgin olive oil

1 tablespoon red chili pepper flakes

1 teaspoon oregano flakes

DIRECTIONS

Cut loaves of bread in half. Layer one side of each loaf with all ingredients.

Mix oil, oregano and red pepper, then sprinkle one tablespoon of oil on each sandwich. Heat under the broiler for 2 minutes. Then top sandwiches with chopped green salad. Serve hot.

Make 6 sandwiches.

<Enjoy! Emilia>

TORTARELLE IN CARROZZA DI CALABRIA

Calabrian Fried Sandwiches

INGREDIENTS

10 slices white bread

10 slices American cheese

10 slices Prosciutto cotto or ham

3 eggs, beaten

3 tablespoons milk

1 cup breadcrumbs

½ cup vegetable oil

DIRECTIONS

Top five bread slices with 1 slice cheese and 1 slice ham. Top with remaining pieces of bread and cut sandwiches in half to form triangles.

Beat eggs and milk together, dip sandwiches into egg/milk mixture, then into breadcrumbs. In non-stick frying pan heat oil and fry triangles until each side is golden brown.

Do not over fry. Transfer sandwiches onto a dish covered with paper towels.

Serve hot for lunch.

Makes 5 servings.

<Enjoy! Emilia>

COLAZIONE ITALIANA CON ARROSTO DI MANZO

Spicy Italian Roast Beef Sandwiches

INGREDIENTS

1 pound Italian roast beef, sliced

8 slices provolone cheese

4 hot vinegar cherry peppers, seeded and chopped

4 tablespoons extra virgin olive oil

¼ teaspoon dry oregano flakes

4 tablespoons onion minced

4 one-foot long Italian rolls cut in half

DIRECTIONS

In a small dish add oil, diced peppers, oregano and mix well. Divide the roast beef into four portions, then pile the roast beef over half of a roll, add provolone cheese, one tablespoon minced onion, and 1 tablespoon of the spiced oil. Cover the sandwiches with top roll and serve.

Makes 4 servings.

<Buon Appetito! Emilia>

POLLO ALLA PARMIGIANA

Chicken Parmesan Sandwiches

INGREDIENTS

4 king rolls

4 pieces of broiled or grilled chicken breast

1 cup marinara sauce

1 cup shredded mozzarella cheese

4 tablespoons Parmesan cheese, grated

DIRECTIONS

Cut bread in half lengthwise and place open faced on a piece of aluminum foil. Place chicken breast on four of the halves, top with marinara sauce and sprinkle with the Parmesan and mozzarella cheeses.

Preheat the oven broiler and broil for 2 minutes or until mozzarella cheese is melted.

Makes 4 servings.

<Enjoy! Emilia>

COLAZIONE ELEGANTE

Classic Sandwiches

INGREDIENTS

1 pound sauerkraut

2 tablespoons Thousand Island dressing

8 slices of dark rye bread

1 pound corned beef, sliced thin

4 slices Swiss cheese

2 tablespoons softened butter

DIRECTIONS

Drain, but do not rinse, the sauerkraut and mix with Thousand Island dressing. Top four slices of bread with sauerkraut mixture, followed by 4oz. of corned beef, one slice of Swiss cheese and coat the outside bread with soft butter.

Grill on both sides until warmed through and cheese melts. Serve hot.

Makes 4 sandwiches.

<Enjoy! Emilia>

COLAZIONE ALLA FRUTTA

Fruit Sandwich

INGREDIENTS

8 oz. soft Italian cheese (mascarpone) or cream cheese

1 teaspoon lemon juice

1 tablespoon sugar

1 tablespoon heavy cream

¼ cup green seedless grapes

¼ cup red seedless grapes

2 pears, peeled and cut into 12 slices

6 croissants

DIRECTIONS

Mix cheese, lemon juice, sugar and heavy cream in a small bowl. Cut croissants in half, divide and spread cheese evenly, add 2 slices of pear on each half of the croissant and top with green and red grapes.

Cover sandwich with other half of the croissant. Serve with a glass of juice, coffee or tea.

<Enjoy! Emilia>

COLAZIONE DI MALENZANI E RICOTTA FRESCA

Eggplant and Fresh Ricotta Sandwiches

INGREDIENTS

3 long eggplants, peeled and sliced round (about 1/2 inch thick)

3 eggs

½ teaspoon salt

¼ teaspoon ground black pepper

1 ½ cups seasoned Italian breadcrumbs

½ pound (8 oz.) fresh ricotta cheese

2 tablespoons Parmesan cheese, ground

1 teaspoon Italian parsley, chopped

1 ½ cup marinara sauce, see recipe to make your own

DIRECTIONS

Preheat oven to 400 F.

In a large bowl add beaten eggs, salt and black pepper. Dip each slice of eggplant first into eggs and then into breadcrumbs. Cover large baking sheet with aluminum foil or parchment paper. Bake in preheated oven for 5 minutes, then turn the eggplant slices over and bake for 5 more minutes, or until eggplants turn golden and crisp.

Meanwhile, mix ricotta, 1 tablespoon Parmesan cheese, with parsley and a pinch black pepper.

When done baking, add half of the marinara sauce to the bottom of a baking pan, then layer half of the eggplant slices, then spoon the ricotta mixture over the eggplant. Top with remaining eggplant slices, and then spoon remaining marinara sauce over each eggplant.

Top with remaining Parmesan cheese, then bake for 5 minutes until the ricotta cheese is good hot.

<Buon Appetito! Emilia>

2. SALADS AND DRESSINGS

INSALATA SICILIANA

Sicilian Salad

INGREDIENTS

2 oranges, sliced

8 leaves Romaine lettuce

8 small slices smoked salmon

24 pitted black olives

4 teaspoons olive oil

1 tablespoon orange juice

1 tablespoon lemon juice

1 pinch salt and pepper

4 slices white bread

DIRECTIONS

Cut orange rind close to the oranges, slice into very thin 'wheels' and cover plates with the orange slices. Then lay two leaves of Romaine on each dish and two rolled up pieces of the smoked salmon. Decorate the top of each salad with 6 olives.

In a small bowl mix oil, lemon juice, orange juice, and salt. Drizzle 1 teaspoon of the juice mixture over each dish.

Cut the slices of bread diagonally in half and lay two triangles of bread on the sides of each dish.

Serve as a brunch, lunch or side salad.

<Enjoy! Emilia>

INSALATA DI FRUTTA

Citrus Salad

INGREDIENTS

3 large seedless grapefruit

3 large navel oranges

3 seedless tangerines

½ cup red raspberries

½ teaspoon lemon juice

12 mint leaves

DIRECTIONS

Peel oranges, the grapefruit and tangerines. Cut and section fruit to remove membranes. Do this over the bowl and let fruit sections fall into bowl, then squeeze remaining juice from the membranes. Add lemon juice and toss gently.

Transfer fruit into six small bowls. Divide raspberries into equal portions and garnish each bowl with two mint leaves.

Makes 6 servings.

<Enjoy! Emilia>

INSALATA MISTA

Citrus Tossed Salad

INGREDIENTS

6 cups torn salad greens

2 grapefruit, peeled, sectioned and seeded

3 oranges, peeled, sectioned and seeded

1 medium red onion, sliced into rings

¼ cup balsamic vinegar

DIRECTIONS

Add all the fruit and salad into large bowl mix gently. Add balsamic vinegar and toss well. Top with onion slices. (You can also use your own vinaigrette instead.)

The following recipe is for basic citrus vinaigrette. You can add the spices you like best.

Makes 6 side dish servings.

<Have fun! Emilia>

CONDIMENTO PER L'INSALATA

Citrus Vinaigrette

INGREDIENTS

1 ½ cup (12 oz.) frozen orange juice concentrate, thawed

½ cup red wine vinegar

½ cup extra virgin olive oil

½ cup water

½ teaspoon ground black pepper

DIRECTIONS

Add all the ingredients in a jar and shake well. Chill for up 1 week. Let stand at room temperature for about 15 minutes before using and shake well.

If you like garlic citrus vinaigrette, then add 2 cloves of crushed garlic or ½ teaspoon garlic powder.

For ginger-citrus vinaigrette, add ½ teaspoon of fresh chopped gingerroot.

For herbed citrus vinaigrette, add ½ teaspoon basil leaf flakes and ½ teaspoon oregano flakes.

All of these homemade vinaigrettes can be refrigerated for 1 week.

Makes 3 cups of dressing.

<Enjoy! Emilia>

EMILIA CONDIMENTO PER L`INSALATA

Emilia Condiments For Salads

INGREDIENTS

1 ½ cup olive oil extra virgin

1 cup rose` wine vinegar

2 clove garlic peel and mince

1 teaspoon salt

½ teaspoon oregano flakes

½ teaspoon dry parsley

½ teaspoon dry basil leaves

2 tablespoons fresh great Parmesan cheese

DIRECTIONS

In a jar with a thigh lid, combine all the ingredients: and shake well.

Refrigerate for 1 day before serve over the salad.

This salad dressing can be poured over green salad, or over potatoe salad.

Can be kept into the refrigerator for 1 week. Shake well before serving.

<All the stuff you make in advance, save you time in the kitchen Emilia>

INSALATA DI RISO CON TRE FAGIOLI

Three Bean & Rice Salad

INGREDIENTS

1 cup cooked long grain rice

½ cup red pinto beans

½ cup cannellini beans

½ cup black beans

½ cup chopped red onion

2 tablespoons Italian parsley

½ cup celery, chopped

2 tablespoons Italian parsley finely chopped

½ cup cherry peppers, chopped

½ cup low fat Italian salad dressing

½ cup garlic powder

DIRECTIONS

Combine rice, all beans, peppers, cherry peppers, onion and celery. Pour salad dressing and garlic powder over the rice mixture and gently toss.

Cover and chill for 2 hours before serving.

Makes 5 servings.

INSALATA DI PASTA

Pasta Salad

INGREDIENTS

8 oz. assorted color short pasta, like fusili or penne

1-cup broccoli florets

1 cup cherry tomatoes, cut in half and seeded

½ cup pine nuts

½ cup fresh basil leaves, cut in half

2 tablespoons parsley, chopped

½ teaspoon salt

½ teaspoon ground black pepper

1 cup green and red sweet pepper, sliced in 1 inch pieces

2 tablespoons Italian salad dressing

1 tablespoon balsamic vinegar

DIRECTIONS

Cook pasta according to package directions. When there are four minutes to go before the pasta is ready to drain, add the broccoli florets to the pasta pot. Drain pasta when al dente and broccoli florets are tender.

Return pasta and broccoli to the pot. When pasta mixture is cool add all remaining ingredients.

This dish can be made for family dinner or party. Can also be made a day ahead and stored in the refrigerator before serving.

Makes 4 servings

<Enjoy! Emilia>

INSALATA DI GAMBERI AL LIMONE

Tossed Salad with Shrimp and Lemon Juice

INGREDIENTS

1 pound fresh peeled shrimp

3 cups uncooked white rice

8 cups fresh mixed salad greens

INGREDIENTS FOR THE VINAIGRETTE

¼ cup white wine vinegar

¼ cup lemon juice

3 cups water

1 tablespoon lemon peel

1 cup red onion thinly sliced

2 tablespoons extra virgin olive oil

DIRECTIONS

In a small jar combine all of the ingredients for the vinaigrette. Shake well until blended and refrigerate for 2 hours or until serving time.

Cocking rice according to the package directions. (Always cook rice al dente for a salad.) Let stand 5 minutes, then fluff with a fork. Allow to cool for at least 20 minutes before using in the salad.

While the rice is cooling, sauté shrimp in a small non-stick pan with vegetable spray until the shrimp turn pink, and then let cool for 5 minutes. In a large bowl combine mixed salad greens, cooked rice and shrimp. Pour vinaigrette over the salad and toss well. Serve cool for lunch, a family party or a brunch.

Makes 8 servings.

<Buon Appetito! Emilia>

INSALATA DI POLLO, RISO E ARUGULA

Chicken, Rice & Arugula Salad

INGREDIENTS

2 ½ cups uncooked instant brown rice

4 boneless skinless chicken breast halves

¾ cup pine nuts

10 cups chopped arugula

¼ cup green onions, sliced

¼ cup red onions, sliced

¼ cup red bell pepper, thinly sliced

¼ cup green bell pepper, thinly sliced

¼ cup fresh basil leaves, finely chopped

1-½ cups chicken broth

1-½ cups water

1 cup tomatoes, thinly sliced

FOR THE VINAIGRETTE

1 teaspoon lemon peel

¼ cup lemon juice

½ teaspoon salt

½ teaspoon black pepper

½ cup extra virgin olive oil

2 tablespoons balsamic vinegar

¼ cup blue cheese, crumbled

DIRECTIONS

Add the ingredients for the vinaigrette in a jar, shake well, cover and refrigerate for 2 hours or until it is serving time.

Combine water and broth, bring to a boil, stir in the rice, cover and remove from heat. Let stand 5 to 7 minutes and fluff rice with fork.

While the rice is cooking and cooling, broil the chicken breasts in the oven or on a grill for 5 minutes on each side.

Cut roasted chicken in small strips and mix in a bowl with the vinaigrette, then combine rice and vegetables in a large bowl, mixing well. Then add half of the pine nuts and vinaigrette mixture. Transfer salad mixture onto a serving platter and garnish salad with remaining pine nuts. Refrigerate until serving time.

Makes 6 servings.

<Have fun! Emilia>

INSALATA GRECA

Greek Salad

INGREDIENTS

1 head iceberg lettuce, torn into bite size pieces

2 tomatoes, cut into quarters

½ cup red onion, diced

1 English cucumber, peeled and diced

1 red pepper, diced

1 green pepper, diced

1 pound feta cheese, crumbled

16 oz. Italian herb dressing

8 oz. pitted Greek olives

8 oz. pitted black olives

DIRECTIONS

In a large bowl mix all the ingredients except for olives and feta cheese. Top with crumbled feta cheese and olives.

If you want to assemble the salad ahead of time, do not add the Italian dressing until ready to serve, as this will keep the lettuce crisp.

Make 6 servings.

<Enjoy your meal! Emilia>

INSALATA DI RISO

Wild Rice Salad

INGREDIENTS

1 cup wild rice, uncooked

6 oz. roasted seasoned ham, cut in small cubes

½ cup green onions, chopped

1 cup porcini mushrooms

1 tablespoon fresh basil, chopped

FOR THE VINAIGRETTE

3 tablespoons balsamic vinegar

1 teaspoon oregano flakes

½ teaspoon salt

1 tablespoon Italian parsley, chopped

1 teaspoon dried rosemary flakes

DIRECTIONS

Cook rice according to package directions and transfer into large bowl.

(Cool for at least 20 minutes before adding all of the rest of the salad ingredients to the rice.)

Add the ingredients for the vinaigrette in a jar, shake well, cover and refrigerate for 2 hours or until it is serving time.

Mix all the remaining ingredients and add the vinaigrette. Chill for 1 hour before serving.

Makes 6 servings.

<It is fun to try all kinds of different European salads and meals. Emilia>

CONDIMENTO D'INSALATA AL GORGONZOLA

Blue Cheese Salad Dressing

INGREDIENTS

1 pound blue cheese, broken into pieces

3 cloves of garlic, peeled and crushed

2 cups mayonnaise

2 teaspoons parsley, finely chopped

½ teaspoon fresh ground black pepper

DIRECTIONS

Reserve ½ cup of the blue cheese and set aside. Place the remaining cheese into a medium size bowl and beat with electric mixer until smooth. Then add all remaining ingredients and beat together until salad dressing is thick, smooth and creamy. Stir in remaining crumbled cheese.

Spoon over cold crisp salad greens. This may also be used as a dip and will keep refrigerated for up to 2 weeks.

Makes about 4 cups of dressing.

<Have fun! Emilia>

CONDIMENTO PER L'INSALATA CON IL MIELE

Blue Cheese Salad Dressing With Honey

INGREDIENTS

1 tablespoon balsamic vinegar

3 tablespoons honey mustard

1 tablespoon water

¼ cup olive oil

DIRECTIONS

Stir vinegar, honey mustard and water together until blended. Add olive oil and serve over your favorite salad or use as a marinade for chicken before grilling.

<Enjoy! Emilia>

INSALATA CON POCO SODIOM

Eat-light Lower Sodium Chef Salad

INGREDIENTS

5 cups of romaine or leaf lettuce

1 cup fresh mushrooms

1 cup cucumber slices

2 small onions, sliced

4 oz. low sodium Muenster cheese

2 oz. low sodium bologna

2 oz. low sodium ham

6 oz. low sodium turkey

6 oz. low sodium roast beef

¼ cup red bell pepper slices

1 cup asparagus, blanched and cut into 2 inch pieces

DIRECTIONS

Wash and drain lettuce, place in large salad bowl and add all ingredients except the last two.

Decorate top of salad with slices of red pepper and asparagus. Serve with your favorite low sodium dressing or vinaigrette.

<Enjoy! Emilia>

SALMONE ALLA GRIGLIA PER L`INSALATA

Grilled Salmon Salad

INGREDIENTS

Croutons:

2 cups Italian bread, cubed

1 teaspoon garlic powder

Salad:

2 salmon fillets, 1 ½ pound each

2 cups romaine lettuce, torn

1 cup arugula, torn

1-½ cups cherry tomatoes

Vinaigrette:

2 tablespoons olive oil

¼ cup balsamic vinegar

4 cloves of garlic, peeled and minced

2 tablespoons lemon juice

½ teaspoon salt

½ teaspoon ground black pepper

1 teaspoon sugar

4 tablespoons shaved Parmesan cheese

DIRECTIONS

For croutons, put bread cubes on a cookie sheet, spray with vegetable or olive oil, sprinkle garlic powder and bake in the oven for 3 minutes each side.

Coat salmon with vegetable or olive oil.

Place salmon with skin side down on the grill. Grill on low-medium heat for 10 minutes. Let salmon cool for a few minutes and flake it into salad size chunks.

In small bowl mix the olive oil, balsamic vinegar, pinch salt and black pepper and sugar.

In a large bowl mix all salad ingredients and then add croutons and salmon chunks. Add dressing over the salad, toss, and add Parmesan cheese.

Makes 4 servings.

<Have fun! Emilia>

INSALATA MISTA

Tossed Salad

INGREDIENTS

Salad:

2 tablespoons red onion, shredded

½ cup carrots, shredded

2 medium bunches romaine, torn

4 oz. provolone cheese, cut into thin strips

Vinaigrette:

1 tablespoon wine vinegar

¼ cup balsamic vinegar

½ teaspoon salt

½ teaspoon ground black pepper

¼ teaspoon dried oregano flakes

½ cup extra virgin olive oil

DIRECTIONS

In a small bowl, combine, wine vinegar, balsamic vinegar, salt and pepper, oregano and mix well with a fork. Add oil and mix well.

In a large salad bowl combine all salad ingredients then gently toss the salad.

Pour dressing over the salad and toss very lightly again.

Makes 10 servings.

<Have fun! Emilia>

EMILIA INSALATA DI PESCE

Emilia's Seafood Salad

INGREDIENTS

2 ½ pounds mussels

1 pound shrimps

½ pound small squid

½ pound catfish

½ pound octopus

½ cup lemon juice

½ teaspoon hot red pepper flakes

½ teaspoon salt

½ teaspoon ground black pepper

2 cloves of garlic, peeled and chopped

2 tablespoons parsley, chopped

DIRECTIONS

The secret to this dish is in the preparation.

Cut squid and catfish into small pieces, about the same size as the mussels, and makes sure that all the seafood is washed and cut well. It should then all be cooked lightly with olive oil for 10 minutes and then and seasoned with salt, pepper, garlic, lemon juice and red hot pepper flakes.

Sauté for another 10 minutes on low heat, transfer to a serving platter and garnish with parsley.

You can serve this dish over cooked rice, cool or warm.

<Buon Appetito! Emilia>

INSALATA DI PATATE PER LA FESTA

Party-sized Vinaigrette Potato Salad

INGREDIENTS

3 pounds small new white potatoes

¾ cup diced green pepper, diced

¾ cups green onion, thinly sliced

¾ cup minced fresh parsley, minced

½ cup extra virgin olive oil

½ cup red wine vinegar

1 lemon zest

1 teaspoon lemon juice

½ teaspoon salt

½ teaspoon ground black pepper

DIRECTIONS

Wash and scrub potatoes, boil, unpeeled, until tender about 25 to 30 minutes. Do not overcook. Drain and cut potatoes into quarters and arrange in large glass dish. Add green peppers, onions and sprinkle with parsley.

In a jar with a tight fitting lid, combine oil, vinegar, salt and pepper, lemon zest and lemon juice. Shake well and pour dressing over vegetables while potatoes are still warm. Toss gently. Let salad marinate for 1 hour at room temperature before serving.

Makes 18 servings.

<Have fun! Emilia>

SALSA TARTARA

Vinaigrette Sauce

INGREDIENTS

2 hard-boiled egg yolks

2 tablespoons olive oil

2 oz. cappers, packed in vinegar

1 oz. pickles in vinegar

2 tablespoons fresh lemon juice

¼ teaspoon ground black pepper

1 pinch salt

DIRECTIONS

In small bowl mash eggs yolks with a fork, then add oil one tablespoon at time. Add capers, pickles, and lemon juice and add salt and pepper.

Refrigerate for four hours before use. If you don't need the sauce the same day, it will keep for two days in the refrigerator.

Serve over your favorite meats or fish.

<Have fun! Emilia>

3. VEGETABLE SIDES

VEGETALI PER IL CONTORNO CON I SAPORI DI CALABRIA

Vegetable Sides with a Southern Italian Taste

Broccoli and Broccoli Rape: These two vegetables are from the same family, but have very different tastes. Broccoli has a very mild taste and broccoli rape has a bitter taste. Both can be boiled or steamed.

Salad and other greens: Southern Italy is the best land of salad and greens. Almost anything that grows in the garden can be used in the kitchen for one meal or another.

Arugula: A green Mediterranean lettuce that can also be used in a risotto dish or in minestrone soup.

Escarole: This green lettuce is firm crisp and slightly bitter.

Escarole can be use in salad, soup or minestrone with pasta and beans.

Tomatoes: An important part of the Italian cuisine. Canned, whole, diced, crush, or pureed they are use for sauce, soups or minestrone, pizzaiola and bruschetta, just to name a few things. Look for Italian brands. Pastine means kitchen ready with no salt added. Progresso, Rienzi and Barilla are other brands. Crushed tomatoes can be use in pizzaiola; plum tomatoes are the best for salad and antipasti.

Italian cooking wouldn't be the same without tomatoes!

Oregano: Oregano is the most used spice in Italian dishes, and even more so in the south of Italy, to season pizza toppings, sauces and vegetables.

Sage: Used to flavor pork, meats, lamb, potatoes and even some other dishes if you like the flavor.

Eggplant: It is hard to imagine cooking Calabrian without this wonderful vegetable. It can be stuffed, roasted, used in the sauce over the pasta dish or grilled.

Zucchini: A wonderful summer vegetable. It is like eggplant in that it gives you plenty of meals and side dishes with good flavor.

Italian Parsley: This parsley has flat leaves and has more flavor then the curly parsley. It can be used for Italian meatballs, salad and to garnish dishes.

Onion: A delicious flavor when added to soups, sauces, salads, salad dressing, and minestrone soup.

Garlic: Use peeled, chopped or minced. It can be bought at supermarkets minced in a small container and needs to be refrigerated. You can also buy garlic powder, but the flavor is not the same. In Southern Italy, garlic is the number one spice used in food. When browning garlic, be very careful with the hot oil and always make the garlic golden brown.

Basil Leaves: Fresh basil is a popular Italian herb used to make pesto sauce and season tomato salads, marinara sauce, primavera, and is often used over pasta dishes as a garnish.

The Italian tradition of combining herbs and spices is the best for adding flavor to your dish. On occasion you may not have fresh herbs, and you can substitute dry herbs and spices. This will work just as well.

When I cook for myself I use lots of spice, because this gives flavor to the food and I do not have to use salt. Celery is one vegetable that is commonly used as a substitute for salt, and the combination of parsley and fresh basil will give you a good taste without adding salt to a dish.

Imagine your kitchen filled with this beautiful aroma from herbs and spices. Sometimes it involves unusual combinations, like lemon with herbs and spice give you the best aroma in your kitchen and in your meals.

You don't need a passport to taste fabulous flavors from faraway land like Southern Italy. All supermarkets and grocery stores are now filled with Italian herbs and spices.

<Enjoy this adventure! Emilia>

PEPERONI E MALENZANI SOTTO ACETO

Peppers & Eggplant Preserved in Vinegar

INGREDIENTS

6 large bell red peppers

6 Italian eggplants

6 cups white vinegar

4 cups water

2 tablespoons salt

6 cloves of garlic, peeled and chopped

1 cup capers

½ cup olive oil

1 cup vegetable oil if needed

DIRECTIONS

Wash, core and seed peppers, then wash eggplant, cutting off the top and bottom. Slice into long thin strips.

In a large deep saucepan add vinegar, water, and salt. Bring to a boil, add peppers strips and let boil for 30 to 40 seconds. Drain using a spatula into a colander in order to drain the excess liquid. Put the peppers over towel paper to dry well. Then add eggplant strips and boil for 30 seconds, draining the same way as with the peppers.

When peppers and eggplant strips are cool, put all into a big bowl, add oregano, chopped garlic, olive oil and cappers, toss well. Spoon eggplant and peppers into a Mason jar and cover with oil. You may need more than 1 cup of oil. Seal jars and store in the refrigerator. The vegetables are ready to be eaten after 3 weeks.

This makes a good antipasto next to cheese and salami.

<Have fun! Emilia>

MIA MAMMA POMODORI SECCHI

My Mother's Sun Dried Tomatoes

INGREDIENTS

5 pounds of ripe plum tomatoes

2 tablespoons salt

½ cup fresh basil chopped

Olive oil to cover the dried tomatoes

DIRECTIONS

Wash tomatoes and then cut lengthwise, leaving tomatoes attached at the end. Cover large baking sheet with aluminum foil: set a rack on top. Place tomatoes on top with cut side up, and sprinkle with salt. If you have a back yard or a closed porch, let tomatoes dry for 2 days, then preheat oven at 300 F and bake for 20 minutes: then open oven door 2 inch and bake for 2 hours. Do not allow them to burn.

When tomatoes are done, let cool then put into sterilized jars. On the top add some of the chopped basil and cover with olive oil, enough to cover the tomatoes. Seal and store in the refrigerator: but after 24 hours open the jars and make sure the top is still covered with the oil, if not add little more.

Makes about 2 pints.

<Have fun! Emilia>

PEPERONI ROSSI ARROSTITE

Roasted Red Peppers

INGREDIENTS

6 large red bell peppers

DIRECTIONS

Place rack in a broiler pan, heat broiler at high temperature, place rack in the oven, under the broiler, as the peppers begin to blister: use a tong to turn the peppers over; each side should have an even blister. Remove from the oven and cover peppers with brown paper bags. Let the peppers cool for 5 minutes, and then remove the skin and seeds.

Slice the peppers ½ thick lengthwise; lay them over paper towels to dry. Put peppers into a small bowl; add olive oil, garlic and chopped Italian parsley. To freeze: cut peppers into halve, after the peppers dry, put them into a plastic freezer bags. You can freeze for up to 6 months. When you need them, defrost 3 hours in advance, dry over paper towels and serve over pasta dishes, bruschettas, or for a side dish.

<Enjoy! Emilia>

FUNGHI PORTABELLO E PATATE ALLA GRIGLIA

Grilled Portabello Mushrooms and Potatoes

INGREDIENTS

4 large Russet potatoes

2 large Portabello mushrooms

5 teaspoons extra virgin olive oil, divided

1 teaspoon balsamic vinegar

¼ teaspoon salt

¼ teaspoon ground black pepper

1 cup onion, thinly sliced

1 cup green pepper, thinly sliced

¼ cup dry white wine

½ teaspoon dried oregano flakes

1 cup tomato, finely diced

DIRECTIONS

Wash potatoes thoroughly with a brush, so that the skin may be eaten. Pierce several times with a fork and bake in a preheated oven at 425 F. for 50 minutes.

Remove stem from mushrooms, chop and reserve. Combine 1 tablespoon of the oil, vinegar, half of the salt and pepper, and brush mushroom caps with mixture. Grill or broil, rounded side up, about 4 inches from heat, for 2 minutes or until mushrooms are thoroughly heated. Set aside.

Sauté mushroom stems, onion and green pepper in remaining oil and vinegar mixture, with oregano, salt and pepper to taste. Sauté until wine is absorbed, then add tomatoes and heat thoroughly. Cut top of potatoes lengthwise. Squeezes end push toward center to open. Slice grilled mushrooms and arrange on potatoes. Spoon ¼ of vegetable mixture on top of each mushroom.

Makes 4 servings.

<Have fun! Emilia>

TORTA DI ZUCCHINI DA ZIA GIUSEPPINA

My Aunt Josephine's Zucchini Pie

INGREDIENTS

3 cups finely shredded zucchini

4 eggs, beaten

1 cup biscuit mix (like Bisquick)

2 tablespoons Parmesan cheese, grated

2 tablespoon Romano cheese, grated

¾ cup fontina cheese, shredded

¼ cup extra virgin olive oil

¾ cup yellow onion, minced

2 tablespoons parsley, chopped

¼ teaspoon salt

½ teaspoon ground black pepper

DIRECTIONS

Preheat oven to 375 F.

In a large bowl combine all the ingredients from the recipe, and mix well with hand mixer on low speed.

Grease 9-inch baking dish. Add the mixture and bake for 40 minutes.

Insert a toothpick or piece of spaghetti in the center of the pie. If spaghetti comes out clean from the pie dough, then the pie is done. If dough clings to the spaghetti, then bake for 5 to 10 minutes longer.

Serve as side dish, or cut in small pieces for a party appetizer tray.

Thank you Aunt Josephine!

ZUCCHINE AL FORNO

Scalloped Zucchini

INGREDIENTS

4 small Italian zucchini

1 cup whipping cream

¼ cup milk

½ teaspoon ground black pepper

2 cloves of garlic, peeled and minced

1 cup fontina cheese, shredded

½ cup Parmesan cheese, grated

½ teaspoon salt

DIRECTIONS

Preheat oven to 375 F. and spray a baking dish with vegetable oil spray, or grease an ovenproof skillet with ½ teaspoon softened butter and set aside.

Wash zucchini, pat dry with paper towel, and cut them into ¼ inch rounds. In a small saucepan combine cream and milk and beat until puffy. Add salt, black pepper and garlic. Layer half the zucchini in greased dish, top with half the mixture and half of the cheese. Repeat layer with zucchini, the cream mixture, and top with the remaining cheese.

Bake uncovered for 10 minutes. The zucchini should be tender and the cheese melted. Let stand 4 minutes before serving. Serve with a rice dish or as a side dish with baked chicken.

This recipe can also be made with potatoes instead of zucchini.

Makes 4 servings.

<Buon Appetito! Emilia>

ZUCCHINI RIPIENI DA EMILIA

Emilia's Stuffed Zucchini

INGREDIENTS

5 Italian zucchini, about 6 inches long

2 tablespoons extra virgin olive oil

2 cloves garlic, minced

4 oz. ground turkey

½ teaspoon ground black pepper

1 egg white

½ cup Parmesan cheese, shredded

1 ½ cups seasoned breadcrumbs

¼ teaspoon salt

¾ cup tomatoes, diced

2 tablespoons parsley, chopped

½ cup dry white wine

DIRECTIONS

Preheat oven to 375 F.

Wash, dry and cut zucchini in half lengthwise. Remove the white pulp from zucchini with a melon ball scoop. Cook zucchini shells in boiling salt water for 2 minutes. Drain and set aside.

In a skillet add oil and garlic; sauté until garlic is golden. Add ground turkey, black pepper and cook for 4 minutes at a low simmer, or until turkey is no longer pink. Transfer turkey into a large bowl. Let stand for 5 minutes until meat is cool. Add egg white, grated cheese, parsley, tomatoes, salt, wine and mix thoroughly.

80

Divide mix into the stuffed zucchini shells and place in a greased baking dish. Sprinkle each zucchini with 2 tablespoons of shredded Parmesan cheese and cover dish with foil. Bake for 10 minutes, then uncover and bake for 2 minutes longer to brown the cheese.

Makes 5 servings.

<Buon Appetito! Emilia>

PEPERONI ARROSTITI ALLA CALABRESE

Southern Italian-style Roasted Peppers

INGREDIENTS

6 large peppers 2 red, 2 green, and 2 yellow

2 tablespoons Parmesan cheese, grated

2 tablespoons breadcrumbs

2 cloves of garlic, peeled and chopped

1 tablespoon, fresh basil leaves, chopped

2 tablespoons parsley, chopped

12 anchovies filets in olive oil

1 cup tomatoes, peeled and chopped

3 tablespoons olive oil

½ teaspoon salt

½ teaspoon ground black pepper

DIRECTIONS

Preheat oven to the broil setting.

Wash the peppers, place them in a large baking pan with a grill insert, and put them in the oven under the broiler. Roast until the skins are black, checking the peppers and turning them around frequently so that all sides are blackened. Use tongs so as to not burn your hands. When finished roasting, put peppers into a flat dish, cover with paper towels and allow cooling for 10 minutes.

While waiting for the peppers to cool, combine ground cheese, breadcrumbs, chopped garlic, basil leaves, 1 tablespoon chopped parsley, salt and pepper, chopped and peeled tomatoes, and oil in a small bowl.

Cut the peppers in half to peel and de-seed them, then cut each half in half, which will give you 12 sections of peppers. Lay the pepper sections out on a large flat serving platter. Divided the cheese and herb mixture into 12 portions. Spoon evenly over peppers and decorate top with remaining chopped parsley.

Serve as second dish or over your favorite pasta.

Makes 6 servings.

<Buon Appetito! Emilia>

VEGETALE ASSORTITE RIPIENI

Assorted Stuffed Vegetables

INGREDIENTS

2 Italian zucchini

2 Italian eggplants

2 bell peppers, 1 red and 1 yellow

2 ripe tomatoes

1 cup mushrooms, sliced and already cooked

1 egg

3 tablespoons olive oil

2 tablespoons softened butter

½ teaspoon ground black pepper

½ teaspoon salt

6 slice stale Italian bread

Vegetable oil spray

DIRECTIONS

Preheat oven to 375 F.

Wash and dry all the vegetables. Cut the zucchini and eggplants lengthwise in half and scoop out the soft white insides and save the eggplant pulp in a separate bowl for later. Cut the top off of the tomato and use a spoon or melon boll to take out the seeds and soft insides save in a separate bowl for later use. Cut off the tops of peppers and wash and de-seed them.

In a large saucepot of lightly salted boiling water, add vegetables and cook eggplants, zucchini and pepper for 1 minute. Cut bread into pieces: then put bread into a food processor, give 4 to 5 pulse, this will make good fresh breadcrumbs. Gently get vegetables out of the pan with care not to break and lay them out on a flat serving dish. Chop the reserved insides from eggplants and tomatoes. In a skillet heat 1 tablespoon butter and 1 tablespoon oil, then add chopped garlic, chopped vegetables, black pepper and salt. Sauté on low heat for 2 minutes. Transfer cooked vegetables to a large bowl and add the grated cheese, parsley, breadcrumbs and egg.

Mix well with fork or your hands and scoop the mixture into vegetables. In a large flat baking pan, add ¼ cup water, remaining oil and bake for 30 minutes. Take the pan out from the oven, and then sprinkle some more breadcrumbs over the vegetables and lightly coat with vegetable oil spray. Bake for 10 more minutes, or until the tops of the vegetables turn light brown.

Serve with rice dish or as your favorite side dish.

Makes 14 servings.

<Enjoy! Emilia>

CARCIOFI E PATATE

Artichokes & Potato

INGREDIENTS

12 baby artichokes

6 large potatoes, peeled and cut in 4

1 medium yellow onion, chopped

2 tablespoon parsley, chopped

¼ cup olive oil

½ teaspoon salt

½ teaspoon ground black pepper

¾ cup water

DIRECTIONS

Wash the artichokes, slice off the tops and pull off the outside leaves until you get the white inner leaves this is know as the "heart" of the artichoke. Quarter the artichoke hearts and cook in boiling salted water until they are very tender.

Note: When cleaning artichokes, put them into water with ¼ cup lemon juice. Without this lemon juice treatment the artichokes will turn dark and not look very appetizing.

In a large saucepan add potatoes, artichoke hearts, chopped onions, parsley, salt, pepper and oil. Add ¾ cup water and bring to a boil. Cover and simmer until the potatoes are cooked about 10-12 minutes. Serve as an appetizer.

Makes 6 Servings.

<Have fun! Emilia>

TORTA ALLE ZUCCHINI

Zucchini Pie

INGREDIENTS

4 cups zucchini, shredded

1-½ cup biscuit mix

¾ cup Parmesan cheese, grated

1 cup fontina cheese, shredded

½ cup olive oil

¾ cup yellow onion, minced

2 tablespoons fresh parsley, chopped

5 eggs, beaten

DIRECTIONS

Preheat oven to 375 F. and grease a 9-inch pie pan or ovenproof dish.

In a large bowl mix all of the ingredients above except the eggs with a large spoon or spatula.

In a small bowl, beat the eggs and then mix them thoroughly into the ingredients in the large bowl.

Pour the mixture into the prepared pan and bake for 40 minutes.

Makes 8 servings.

<Have fun! Emilia>

Emilia Fusco

CROCCHETTE DI PAPATE

Potato Croquettes

INGREDIENTS

2-½ pounds of baking potatoes

2 tablespoons butter

1 teaspoon salt

½ cup Romano cheese, grated

1 teaspoon baking powder

2 tablespoons Italian parsley, finely chopped

1 pinch ground black pepper

1-¼ cup flour

3 eggs, beaten

2 cups vegetable oil

1 cup olive oil

DIRECTIONS

Boil potatoes. When they are done, peel and smash them with a rice mill.

In a large bowl make a well in the center of the milled potatoes. Add the butter, salt, cheese, baking powder, parsley, and a pinch of ground black pepper. Mix well, then add eggs and 1 cup the flour and continue mixing until the mixture is of uniform consistency.

Put mixture on a wood surface sprinkled with flour and work the mixture as if you were making bread. Put mixture back into bowl and cover with a dishtowel and let rest for 10 minutes.

90

Cut dough into small pieces and roll about 5 to 6 inches long and round ½ inch; bring together to the ends to make a small circle. Put all on top of a tablecloth until you finish making the croquettes, and then cover for 5 minutes.

In large skillet heat oil until very hot, add ciambelle 4 or 5 at time and turn them until golden. When they are done take them out from the oil and put in a large dish over paper towels to drain the excess oil. Serve hot: if you want a fancy presentation sprinkle powder sugar over the top.

You can also roll the dough into 3 to 4 inch-long pieces for frying instead, as this will save you time.

<This recipe is from my hometown, and I still make it. Enjoy! Emilia>

ZUCCHINE RIPIENI ALLE PATATE

Zucchini Stuffed with Potatoes and Cheese

INGREDIENTS

6 thin Italian zucchini

6 large golden potatoes

½ cup mozzarella, shredded

6 oz. fontina cheese cut in ¼ inch piece

½ cup great Parmesan cheese

½ cup Italian parsley, chopped

1 tablespoon olive oil

1 cup vegetable stock, or chicken broth

DIRECTIONS

Preheat oven to 375 F.

Boil potatoes in pan with salt water until they are very tender. Peel and mash like you would to make mashed potatoes then add shredded mozzarella, ½ Parmesan cheese, parsley, oil, and fontina cheese and set aside.

Wash, dry, and cut zucchini lengthwise, then scoop out the insides. Add zucchini to a large pan of boiling water, let boil for 1 minute and take zucchini out from the pan. Scoop potato and cheese mixture into zucchini and sprinkle remaining Parmesan cheese on top.

In a large baking pan add the stock; put zucchini in the pan, cover with foil and then bake in preheated oven for 25 minutes. Uncover and bake for 5 more minutes. Serve hot with a tossed salad.

Makes 6 servings.

<Enjoy! Emilia>

ZUCCHINI AL POMODORO

Zucchini & Tomato

INGREDIENTS

3 large Italian zucchini, about 2 pounds

4 cloves of garlic, peeled and chopped

1 teaspoon salt

½ teaspoon ground black pepper

¼ cup fresh basil leaves, chopped

2 tablespoons Italian parsley, chopped

1 teaspoon oregano flakes

1 cup tomatoes, peeled

DIRECTIONS

Wash zucchini and trim the ends. Slice into rounds that are less than ½ inch thick. Coat a large skillet with vegetable cooking spray and sauté garlic until golden. Add zucchini and remaining spices. Stir and turn the zucchini so they color nicely on both sides.

Transfers zucchini into a dish, and add the tomatoes to the skillet to cook for 10 minutes on low to medium heat. Add zucchini to the skillet and cook for an additional 4 minutes. Serve hot over rice.

Makes 6 servings.

<Buon Appetito! Emilia>

PATATE AL ROSAMARINO

Rosemary Potatoes

INGREDIENTS

2 ½ pounds of potatoes

½ teaspoon rosemary flakes

1 pinch nutmeg

¼ cup olive oil

3 clove garlic, peeled and chopped

vegetable oil spray

3 sage leaves

DIRECTIONS

Preheat oven to 400 F.

Peel potatoes, wash, dry and cut into 1½ cube. Spray a baking dish with vegetable oil and add potatoes and all ingredients except the sage leaves. Mix well.

Bake in preheated oven for 15 minutes. When potatoes are golden, gently turn them to the other side and bake for 15 minutes longer.

With a large slotted spoon or spatula drain potatoes from oil. Transfer to a serving dish and garnish with sage leaves.

Serve with your favorite meats or fish.

<Buon Appetito! Emilia>

FRITTELLE DI PATATE CON MOZZARELLA

Fried Potatoes with Mozzarella Cheese

INGREDIENTS

3 large potatoes

4 oz. Buffalo mozzarella

¾ cup flour

½ teaspoon salt

¼ teaspoon ground black pepper

2 eggs, beaten

¾ cup plain breadcrumbs

4 anchovy filets packed in oil, coarsely chopped

DIRECTIONS

Peel potatoes, wash, dry and cut into ½ inch rounds. Cut mozzarella cheese into ¼ inch thick slices.

Dip potato slices into flour seasoned with the salt and pepper, then eggs and then breadcrumbs. On each slice of potato place 1 slice of mozzarella cheese, 2 pieces of anchovy, and then cover with another slice of potato.

Heat oil in a frying pan and when very hot, gently add potatoes. Fry until golden, then turn over to fry on the other side. Let cook until golden and light brown. Transfer fried potatoes to a dish with paper towels to dry the excess oil.

Serve hot.

Makes 4 servings.

<Enjoy! Emilia>

MALENZANE TRUFFOLATE AL FORMAGGIO

Truffle Eggplant with Cheese

INGREDIENTS

6 long Italian eggplants

3 cloves of garlic, peeled and chopped

¼ cup extra-virgin olive oil

¼ cup Romano cheese, grated

2 tablespoons plain breadcrumbs

2 tablespoons Italian parsley, chopped

DIRECTIONS

Wash and dry eggplant. Cut into 1 ½ inch thick slices. Heat oil in a non-stick skillet and sauté garlic until light golden. Add diced eggplants, salt and cook for 15 minutes, stirring occasionally so they do not stick to the skillet.

In a small bowl mix cheese, breadcrumbs and parsley. Add to eggplant and stir gently and turn off the heat. Cover skillet for 2 minutes and let mixture set before serving.

For this dish, if you do not like eggplant, diced zucchini can be used instead.

<Enjoy! Emilia>

CAPONATA DI MALENZANE CALABRESE

Calabrian-style Eggplant

INGREDIENTS

1 cup white vinegar

3 cups water

1 teaspoon salt

4 large unpeeled eggplants cut in ¾ inch cubes

2 large green bell peppers, seeded and cut in ¾ inch cubes

1 cup mint, chopped

4 cloves of garlic, peeled and chopped

1 cup onion, minced

¼ cup olive oil

¼ cup basil leaves, chopped

DIRECTIONS

Bring water and vinegar and salt to a boil. Add half the eggplant and pepper cubes and leave in the pan for 1 minute. Drain with spatula or slotted spoon and transfer to a serving bowl. Repeat with the remaining eggplant and pepper cubes.

Let vegetables cool, then combine all remaining ingredients and toss gently. Serve with pork chops and rice.

<Have fun! Emilia>

INSALATA DI VEGETALE ARROSTITE

Roasted Vegetable Salad

INGREDIENTS

3 red bell peppers

3 yellow bell peppers

2 long and thin eggplants

2 long Italian zucchini

1 large bowl assorted salad greens

SALAD DRESSING

1 teaspoon balsamic vinegar

¼ cup wine vinegar

2 teaspoons water

¼ cup extra virgin olive oil

4 oz. crumbled blue cheese

DIRECTIONS

In a large bowl mix the first 4 salad dressing ingredients. Wash and dry all the vegetables. Cut peppers in half and seed. Cut zucchini and eggplants lengthwise, and then into ¼ inch thick slices. Toss vegetables into the salad dressing and coat them thoroughly. Remove the vegetables using a slotted spoon and reserve the dressing.

Grill all the vegetables for 15 minutes, turning vegetables frequently until tender. While vegetables chill, wash the assorted greens and tear into bite sized-pieces. Take the skin off of the red and green peppers with paper towels, then cut into ¼ inch slices as you did with the zucchini and eggplants.

Mix blue cheese into remaining dressing and stir well. Cover bottom of 6 salad plates with salad and divide vegetables into equal portions over the salad. Spoon salad dressing with blue cheese over the top.

Serve as a side dish with your favorite fish or meat main dish.

Makes 6 servings.

<Enjoy! Emilia>

FAGIOLINI VERDE CON ACETO BALSAMIC

Balsamic Green Beans

INGREDIENTS

3 pounds of green beans, both ends trimmed

¾ cup shallots, diced

3 cloves of garlic, peeled and sliced thin

2-½ tablespoons balsamic vinegar

1 pound cherry tomatoes, halved

3-tablespoon extra virgin olive oil

1 tablespoon salt

½ teaspoon ground black pepper

¼ cup fresh Italian parsley, chopped for garnish

DIRECTIONS

Wash beans and cook in a large pot of salted boiling water beans for 10 minutes or until tender. Drain beans in a colander and set aside.

In skillet heat oil, add shallots and sauté for 1 minute. Add sliced garlic and sauté until garlic is golden. Then add cherry tomatoes, salt and pepper and cook for 3 minutes over high heat.

Add the green beans and cook for 4 minutes, tossing or stirring to heat through.

Transfer green beans onto a serving platter, add balsamic vinegar, toss and garnish with fresh chopped parsley.

Makes 6 servings.

<Enjoy! Emilia>

FAGIOLINI INSALATA

Green Bean Salad

INGREDIENTS

2 pounds of green beans, both ends trimmed

½ cup blue cheese, crumbled

¼ cup pine nuts, toasted

1 teaspoon salt

2 tablespoons lemon juice

FOR THE VINAIGRETTE

2 tablespoons red wine vinegar

2 tablespoons extra virgin olive oil

½ teaspoon fresh ground black pepper

¼ cup shallot, finely chopped

½ teaspoon oregano flakes

DIRECTIONS

Wash beans and cook in a large pot of salted boiling water beans for 10 minutes or until tender. Drain beans in a colander and set aside.

Meanwhile, mix all the vinaigrette ingredients in a small bowl and taste for salt and pepper. Cover the bowl with plastic wrap and refrigerate until green beans have cooled down.

Transfer green beans onto a serving platter and add the lemon juice, as this will help preserve the beautiful green color. When beans have cooled down, pour the vinaigrette over the beans and toss gently. Sprinkle the crumbled blue cheese and pine nuts on top to finish the dish.

Serve next to a broiled fish dinner or baked chicken.

<Buon Appetito! Emilia>

COTOLETTE DI POMODORI ROSSI

Red Tomato Cutlets

INGREDIENTS

4 large tomatoes, not too ripe

½ teaspoon salt

1 egg

2 tablespoons skim milk

½ cup fine cornmeal

¼ teaspoon ground black pepper

½ clove of garlic, peeled and finely minced

¼ cup Parmesan cheese, grated

½ cup all-purpose flour

DIRECTIONS

Preheat oven to 400 F.

Wash and dry tomatoes and cut into ¼ inch thick slices. Sprinkle with salt and let drain into a colander for 20 minutes.

In a small bowl beat the egg and milk, then combine cornmeal, black pepper, garlic and cheese into a dish and flour into a second dish. Dip each sliced tomato first into flour, then into egg and last into the cornmeal mixture.

Lay tomatoes flat in a greased baking pan and bake in a preheated oven for 10 minutes. Flip the tomatoes and bake for another 10 minutes, or until golden and light brown. Serve hot or cool.

This dish can be served as side dish or appetizer and can be made with yellow, red or green tomatoes.

<Buon Appetito! Emilia>

4. RISOTO AND POLENTA

RISOTTO DI ASPARACI

Asparagus Risotto

INGREDIENTS

8oz. (1/2 lb.) asparagus spears, trimmed

2 tablespoons extra virgin olive oil

1 tablespoon butter

2 cloves of garlic, peeled and chopped

2 tablespoons minced onions

3 cups chicken broth

2 cups dry white wine

1 pound Arborio rice

¼ teaspoon salt

¼ teaspoon black pepper

DIRECTIONS

Add asparagus to boiling water and cook for 4 minutes. Drain water from the asparagus and set aside.

While the asparagus is cooking, add oil, butter, garlic and onion to a large saucepan and sauté until garlic and onions are golden brown.

Add the 3 cups of chicken broth, wine, rice, salt and pepper. Cover and simmer for 10 minutes. Keep stirring until the risotto absorbs all the liquid and serve topped with the asparagus.

Makes 6 servings.

<Have fun! Emilia>

RISOTTO ALLE ERBE

Herbed Risotto

INGREDIENTS

1 tablespoon extra virgin olive oil

1 tablespoon butter

2 cloves garlic, peeled and chopped

½ cup onions, chopped

1 teaspoon sage, chopped

1 teaspoon rosemary flakes

2 tablespoons chopped parsley

½ cup celery, chopped

1 cup dry white wine

5 cups chicken stock

1 pound Arborio rice

¼ teaspoon salt

¼ teaspoon black pepper

½ cup Parmesan cheese, grated

DIRECTIONS

In a large saucepan, heat oil and butter, add chopped garlic, and sauté garlic until golden brown. Add onions, all of the herbs and seasonings, stock, wine and rice and sauté mixture, stirring constantly: all type of risotto need to be stirring constantly, rice is very easy to get stuck on the bottom of the pan. Cook for 10 to 15 minutes on low heat.

Transfer the rice in a serving dish, and sprinkle with Parmesan cheese. Decorate risotto dish with and additional tablespoon of chopped parsley and serve hot.

Makes 6 servings.

<Enjoy! Emilia>

RISOTTO ALLA MENTE

Minted Risotto

INGREDIENTS

2 tablespoons butter

1 tablespoon olive oil

1 ¼ pound Arborio rice

1 cup dry white wine

8 cups chicken stock

½ pound tomatoes, peeled and chopped into very small cubes

½ cup onion, minced very small

1 heart romaine lettuce, chopped

½ teaspoon salt

¼ teaspoon ground black pepper

¼ cup mint, finely chopped

½ cup grated Parmesan cheese

DIRECTIONS

In a large saucepan heat oil and butter. Add rice and sauté for 2 minutes on low to medium heat. Add wine and let cook at low heat until wine is absorbed. Add chicken stock 2 cups at time. If you do not have chicken stock, you can substitute 2 cups of water and 2 beef bullion cubes for each 2 cups of chicken broth.

When rice is cooked half way, add about 6 cups of liquid into the cooking, add the romaine lettuce, tomatoes, and onion. Add salt, pepper, Parmesan cheese, and mint 1 minute before rice is done. Serve hot.

Makes 6 servings.

<Have fun! Emilia>

RISOTTO ALL TOSCANA

Tuscany Risotto

INGREDIENTS

2 oz. butter

1 small onion, minced

1 pound Arborio rice

½ cup red wine

3 cups chicken stock

2 tablespoons marinara sauce

½ pound chicken livers

1 tablespoon olive oil

½ cup grated Parmesan cheese

DIRECTIONS

In a saucepan heat butter and sauté onion until golden. Add rice and, while stirring constantly, add wine. Stir in the chicken broth slowly and let simmer at low heat. If you think the rice needs more broth, you can add more, or even ½ cup or water.

In a small saucepan boil the chicken livers for 5 minutes. Drain and chop. In a small skillet heat oil and sauté chicken livers for 2 minutes. Add a pinch salt and ground black pepper to taste, and marinara sauce. Add the Parmesan and chicken livers to the risotto. Stir thoroughly and decorate risotto with chopped parsley.

Makes 6 servings.

<Enjoy! Emilia>

COPPA DI RISO AL TONNO E VEGETALI

Rice & Tuna Vegetable Bowl

INGREDIENTS

1 ½ pound Arborio rice

4 tablespoons vinegar

2 tablespoons mayonnaise

3 tablespoons extra virgin olive oil

8 oz tuna packed in oil

1 cup peppers in vinegar chopped

½ cup carrots shredded

½ cup cappers packed in oil

½ cup pitted black olives

½ cup pitted green olives

10 filets anchovy

4 large tomatoes quartered

DIRECTIONS

Cook rice according to package directions. When rice is cocked, drain and rinse under cool water. Let cool completely before you mix with ingredients.

In small bowl mix vinegar, oil and mayonnaise. In large bowl add rice, tuna, carrots, olives peppers and cappers and toss well. If you have a small party, divide rice mixture into 2 bowls.

Add 5 sliced anchovies on top the rice in each bowl, and around the edge use half of the tomatoes in each bowl. Decorate top with chopped parsley.

Makes 12 servings.

<Enjoy you party. Emilia>

ORANGINI DI RISO

Orangini Rice Balls

INGREDIENTS

1 pound cokes Arborio rice

½ cup Romano cheese

¼ teaspoon ground white pepper

½ teaspoon salt

2 tablespoons Italian parsley minced

2 eggs beaten

1 ½ cups breadcrumbs

1 ½ cup vegetables oil for frying

DIRECTIONS

Cook rice according to package direction. Drain well, let cool for 10 minutes and add Romano cheese, white pepper, salt and parsley.

In a flat dish add the breadcrumbs. Add eggs add mix well. Roll 1 ½ tablespoon rice mixture in round balls. Roll rice ball into the breadcrumbs until coated all round.

In large deep fry pan heat oil to 350 F. Fry rice balls until golden and light brown.

Place orangini balls on paper towels to dry the excess oil.

<This can be fun. Enjoy Emilia>

ORANGINI DI RISO RIPIENI

Stuffed Orangini Balls

INGREDIENTS

1 pound Arborio rice

¼ cup melted butter

½ cup onion minced

½ cup ham chopped

½ cup coked peas

½ cup dry white wine

½ teaspoon ground black pepper

½ teaspoon salt

½ teaspoon nutmeg

2 tablespoons parsley finely chopped

2 eggs beaten for the mix

2 eggs beaten for coat the rice ball

1 ½ cup breadcrumbs

¾ cup Romano grated Parmesan cheese

1 ½ cup vegetable oil for frying

1 cup all purpose flour

DIRECTIONS

In large pan with boiling water cook rice according package direction.

Drain well and let cool for 10 minutes. In small saucepan heat butter, add all the ingredients, except the egg, cheese and breadcrumbs, sauté for 2 minutes.

Transfer mixture into a large bowl and add ½ the cheese. Mix rice with eggs and ½ cup cheese. Spoon 1 ½ tablespoon rice into your hand, a roll to a small bowl, makes a small hole in the center with your finger and fill it with the sauté mixture.

Cover the hole with rice a make a round ball. In one dish add flour, in the second dish add eggs beaten, and in the third dish add breadcrumbs. In a skillet heat oil and one at time drop rice ball. Carefully: the oil is very hot.

Remove when rice ball are golden all round. Place the orangini on a paper towel to dry the excess oil.

<This can be fun to make with your family. Have fun Emilia>

TORTA DI RISO

Rice Cake

INGREDIENTS

1 pound zucchini

12 oz Arborio rice

3 eggs beaten

½ cup Parmesan cheese

3 slice American bread crushed

1 tablespoon mint copped

½ teaspoon oregano flakes

½ teaspoon ground black pepper

4 rape tomatoes, peel, seed, and chopped

½ tablespoon salt

3 tablespoons olive oil

DIRECTIONS

Wash and cut zucchini lengthwise, spoon the inside white parts, and cut zucchini in small slice: 1 inch for ¼.

Cook rice according to a package direction. In the last 5 minutes add zucchini to the rice. Drain, rinse with cool water and leave the rice into the colander to drain the excess water. In a small bowl, add bread crushed into chopped tomatoes.

Transfer rice mixture into a bowl add eggs and Parmesan cheese. In small bowl mix oregano, black pepper, American bread, chopped mint, 3 tablespoons oil, and pinch of salt.

Grease a round spring form cake pan, about 9 inches. Add half the rice mixture into the pan, cover with half the tomatoes mixture. Add reaming rice mixture and top with reaming tomatoes mixture.

Bake in preheat oven at 375 F. for 40 minutes. Check the cake after 30 minutes and cover with foil paper. This will avoid the top to turn brown.

This rice cake is good for a small party of first course meals.

<Buon Appetito Emilia>

RISOTTO CON SALCICCIE PICCANTE

Risotto With Hot Sauce

INGREDIENTS

4 links hot Italian sausage, cases remove

5 cups warm water

1 cup dry white wine

½ cup onion finely chopped

2 clove garlic peel and chopped

2 cups Arborio rice

¾ cup grated Parmesan cheese

½ teaspoon salt

¼ teaspoon ground black pepper

2 tablespoons olive oil

2 tablespoons margarine

DIRECTIONS

In a large saucepan heat oil and sauté garlic and onion until golden. Add meats sausage and sauté on low heat until meats is light brown: let wine evaporate and then add rice; stirring frequently until rice is coat with sausage fat.

Reduce heat to low and start adding 1 cup water at time. Continue stirring until water is completely absorbed. Repeat until the rice is cooked, about 20 minutes.

If you need more water add little more. Stir in the butter, and ½ cup the Parmesan cheese. Transfer risotto into a serving dish.

Garnish with remaining cheese. Serve Hot.

<Buon Appetito Emilia>

10 MINUTI POLENTA

Quick Polenta

INGREDIENTS

3 ½ cups water

2 teaspoons salt

10 oz instant corn flour for polenta

2 tablespoons butter

½ cup grate Parmesan cheese

Pam spray

DIRECTIONS

In a medium saucepan bring water to a boiling, and add salt. Add polenta flour 1 cup at time: stirring continually with wood spoon.

Cook for 5 to 6 minutes and keep stirring until the mixture is solid and soft, add Parmesan cheese.

Spray with Pam a large baking rectangle cookie pan. Pour the polenta, and with a flat spatula smooth the top.

Let cool down before cut. This can be cut in small rectangle, square or triangle.

Can be fried or grilled.

<Enjoy Emilia>

POLENTA

Cornmeal Dish

INGREDIENTS

6 cups water

1½ cups fine corn flour

1 teaspoon salt

½ cup grated Parmesan cheese

DIRECTIONS

Dilute 1 cup corn flour and salt into the water while stirring constantly. Set heat on low and keep stirring for 30 minutes If the polenta is too thick, add 1 cup cool water; if it is too watery, add little more corn flour. Polenta should cook for at least 1 hour or more, on low simmer, depending on the quantities you make.

The polenta needs to be stirred from the beginning to the end of the process, and it should be very smooth and thick. Transfer polenta to a large flat platter and pour any sauce you prefer over it. Add Parmesan cheese and serve hot. If you have leftovers, polenta is still good the next day.

<Buon Appetito! Emilia>

POLENTA CON BROCCOLI DI RAPE

Polenta with Fried Broccoli Rapi

INGREDIENTS

1 polenta recipe

1 bunch broccoli rapi

2 tablespoons olive oil

2 cloves garlic, peeled and chopped

1 teaspoon salt

2 tablespoons butter

1 ½ cup fontina cheese, shredded

¼ cup Parmesan cheese, grated

DIRECTIONS

Thoroughly wash the rapi, take the big stems out and chop into large pieces.

Heat oil in a small saucepan, then sauté chopped garlic until golden. Add rapi, a pinch salt and steam for 5 minutes, stirring and cooking until tender. Transfer rapi into a colander to drain all the excess liquid using a spatula to press down, as you want the rapi as dry as possible for the polenta.

In a baking dish dissolve butter and place half of the polenta in the dish. Spread half the fontina and Parmesan cheeses, and then spoon the rapi over the cheeses. Cover top with remaining shredded fontina cheese. Bake uncovered for 15 minutes or until cheese is lightly golden brown. Serve hot.

This type of polenta can be cut into 2 x 2 inch squares for serving.

Makes 6 servings.

<Enjoy! Emilia>

5. BREADS AND DOUGHS

PANE CASARECCIO DI CALARIA COME LO FACEVA MAMMA

Calabria Homemade Bread Just Like My Mother Used to Make

INGREDIENTS

10 lbs. all-purpose flour

10 cups warm water

1 tablespoon salt

3 active dry yeast packets (¼ oz./7g each)

DIRECTIONS

In a small bowl add 2 cups warm water and the dry yeast. Mix well with your hand.

Put all of the flour and salt in a large bowl and make well in the center, then pour the water and yeast mixture into the well one cup at a time.

Mix using bold hand movements, and once you have formed nice dough, knead it for 2 minutes. Cover for 5 minutes and let the dough rest. This will make dough easy to work with your hands.

If dough is too soft, add little flour. If it is too dry add more warm water.

Work the dough for a good 5 to 8 minutes, then cover with a tablecloth and set in a warm place to rise for 2 ½ hours.

Grease and flour six 9 x 11 pans and put them aside.

Place the dough on a floured surface, and divide dough into 6 portions. Work gently with your hands to make rectangular loaves.

Put each loaf of dough into a greased pan and put all of the pans on a table.

Cover with a tablecloth or a blanket, and let rise for one hour.

Preheat the oven to 450 F.

When you are ready to bake, use two racks in the oven one high and one low. Bake loaves for 20 minutes at 450 F. Then transfer the loaf on the top shelf to the bottom shelf and the loaf on the bottom shelf to the top shelf. Turn the heat down to 400 F. and bake for another 20 minutes. Then lower the temperature again to 375 F. and continue baking for another 20 minutes.

In my hometown each family had a big wood oven, and we made batches of dough from 20 to 30 pounds of flour.

Today I use the stove, and the most I can bake is a recipe for 10 pounds of flour.

This is the bread we eat in our family daily meals.

You can cut down on the recipe: make half or ¼ and divide the ingredients.

This bread is still good like when I was 12 years old, and my Mother made me mix 20-pound batches of flour.

This is my home recipe! You do not have to make 10 pounds flour. For the first time make 2 ½ pound; and divide the remaining ingredients.

<It was hard for me, but the family tradition must to go on. Emilia>

Emilia Fusco

VARIAZIONE DI PANE

Variations of Bread

128

PANE CASARECCIO SCURO

Homemade Wheat Bread

INGREDIENTS

2 pounds wheat flour

1 ½ cups all purpose flour

4 cups warm water

½ teaspoon salt

1 envolop dry yeast

DIRECTIONS

Directio as (HOMEMADE BREAD) on page 104.

When I make the wheat bread, I use the all purpose flour.

Remember: you can make so many different types of bread, Use your immagination, and make what you like best.

When add the warm water, add one cup at time, if the dough is to hard to work with your hand add little more water, if is to soft add little more flour.

PANE CASARECCIO CON ULIVE NERE E PROSHIUTTO

Homemade Bread With Prosciutto and Black Pitted Olives

INGREDIENTS

2 pound wheat flour

1 pound all purpose flour for bread.

3 cups water

½ teaspoon salt

DIRECTIONS ON PAGE 104.

8 oz Prosciutto cut in small cubes, about ¼ inches, 1 cup chopped pitted olive, or you can buy the olives chopped in the can.

To Make the dough use the recipe above. When you mix the flour add the olives and Prosciutto.

Bake as on page 104.

When bread is cooling down: slice and serve. You can make crouton for salad, slice for bruschetta, or eat like regular bread. Any way you eat this bread, it is delicous.

<Have fun!Emilia>

FOCACCIA ALLE ALICE

Anchovy Focaccia

INGREDIENTS

1 pound pizza dough

1 tablespoon olive oil

4 anchovy filets, chopped

2 cloves of garlic, minced

2 tablespoons Parmesan cheese, grated

1 tablespoon parsley, chopped

DIRECTIONS

Preheat oven to 375 F.

Roll out dough into a 9-inch circle about ½ inch thick. Make light cuts in the dough (pizza style) dividing into 8 wedged shaped portions. Grease pizza pan with spray oil: sprinkle with corn meal to stop the dough from sticking to the bottom. Mix oil, chopped anchovy and minced garlic, and spread mixture over dough.

Sprinkle parsley and Parmesan cheese. Bake for 20 minutes or until top is light golden and puffed.

(You can make a Sicilian pizza with this recipe. The Sicilian Pizza is thick like the focaccia. Put your ingredients over the pizza, and bake the same as focaccia.

<Have fun and enjoy. Emilia>

GRESSINI CON IL FORMAGIO ALL`AGLIO

Cheddar Cheese & Garlic Bread Sticks

INGREDIENTS

2 pounds pizza dough

2 cups cheddar cheese, shredded

½ cup garlic, minced

2 tablespoons cornmeal flour

DIRECTIONS

Preheat oven to 350 F.

Roll out dough into a large thin circle. Mix cheese and garlic, spread ½ the cheese and onion over the dough. Fold the dough to cover, and then mix and roll into a circle.

Spread remaining cheese mix over a flour work surface. Cut long strips rolled into 12 inch long and ½ inch thick. Roll dough into round sticks and gently flatten and twist with your fingers – right hand to the right and left hand to the left. Then sprinkle remaining cheese and garlic mixture.

Prepare oven tray: cut piece of waxed paper or parchment paper large enough to cover the tray, and then spread corn meal, as this will stop the cheese from sticking to the paper. Bake in preheated oven for 20 minutes.

Serve with your favorite soup or a chili with beans.

<If you want to change the flavor, use minced onion, rosemary, or fennel seeds.

<Buon Appetito Emilia>

PANA PANICULU

Spiced Corn Bread-My Hometown Recipe

INGREDIENTS

1 pound fine corn flour

1 pound all purpose flour

1 teaspoon salt

1 tablespoon hot red pepper flakes

½ teaspoon oregano flakes

2 tablespoons olive oil

2 cups warm water

1 envelope dry yeast

DIRECTIONS

In a medium bowl add corn flour and purpose flour. Make a well in the center and add salt, red pepper, oregano and oil. Mix well and add and add 1 cup of warm water. Mix the dough and if needed add more water ½ cup at time.

Knead the dough for 5 minutes, then put back in the bowl and cover with a dishcloth. Put the bowl in a warm place, cover with warm blanket and let stay for 2 hours or until the dough has doubled in size. (Corn flour typically needs less time to rise than regular flour.)

Sprinkle flour over a wood surface and divide the dough into 2 portions and put in two greased baking pans of about 7 to 8 inches round. Cover with towel and warm blanket and let the dough rise for 1 hour. Bake bread in a preheated oven at 400F. for 1 hour.

This bread you can eat sliced as is or toast with butter. This can be made plain, without the spice and oregano.

In my town this type bread was made all the time when people were very poor. Today this bread is eaten like a desert.

<From my town to your table. Enjoy! Emilia>

PIZZA BIANCA FACILE

White Easy Pizza

INGREDIENTS

1 package active dry yeast

1 cup warm water

½ teaspoon salt

2 tablespoons olive oil

2 ¾ cups all-purpose flour

1 tablespoon cornmeal

DIRECTIONS

Dissolve yeast in warm water in a warmed mix bowl, and salt, and olive oil. In a mix bowl add flour, make a well in the center and add water mix.

With your hand, work thru the flour and water mixture. Transfer dough over a surface flour place; knead dough for 4 to 5 minutes.

Place dough in a light greased bowl, Cover and let rise in a warm place, free from any draft, for about 2 hours, or until dough doubled in bulk.

Punch dough down. Brush 14 inch pizza pan with oil, or grease with Crisco. Sprinkle with cornmeal. Press dough across bottom of pan, forming a collar around edge to hold toppings.

Add your favor toppings. Bake at 400F. for 15 to 20 minutes.

<When make pizza: have your family help you. This can be fun. Emilia>

PIZZA MARGHERITA

Margarita Pizza

INGREDIENTS

One recipe of Easy Pizza

½ cup marinara sauce

6 basil leaves

6 oz fresh mozzarella cheese thin slice

¼ teaspoon oregano flakes

DIRECTIONS

Spoon the marinara sauce over the pizza, then add mozzarella cheese, basil leaves and sprinkle over the oregano flakes.

Bake at the same direction of easy pizza or until mozzarella is melt.

<Enjoy! This is a good project for the whole family. Emilia>

PIZZA A QUATTRO STAGIONI

Four Season Pizza

INGREDIENTS

1 package dry yeast

1 cup warm water

½ teaspoon salt

2 tablespoons olive oil

3 cups all propose flour

1 tablespoon cornmeal

3/4 cup shredded mozzarella cheese

1 cup tomatoes peel and chopped

6 thin slice pepperoni salami

¼ cup black pitted olive slice

2 thin slice Prosciutto

¼ cup slice mushrooms

DIRECTIONS

Use the method of pizza facile for making the dough for the pizza.

Add over the pizza tomatoes, then with a knife make 4 sections about the top of the pizza. Each section add one the last four ingredients. Sprinkle over the mozzarella cheese.

Bake at preheat oven at 375 F. for 15 to 20 minutes.

Have a pizza night with your family. The children and grandchildren they love to get involved on this project.

For Margarita pizza you want to use only sauce, mozzarella and oregano flakes.

Can been make with anchovy filets. Broccoli rabi, broccoli, zucchini and red and mixed pepper.

<Have fun Emilia>

PANE DOLCE

Sweet Bread

INGREDIENTS

1 cup low fat milk

2 package active dry yeast

¾ cup sugar

2 tablespoons olive oil

½ cup margarine

½ warm water

3 eggs room temperature

7 cup all purpose flour

DIRECTIONS

Place milk, sugar, salt and margarine in a small saucepan. Heat over low heat until margarine melts and sugar dissolves. In a small saucepan heat water to lukewarm.

In a bowl add flour and make a well in the center.

Add warm water and milk mixture to the flour. With your hand work thru all the liquid to the flour. If you think the dough is to soften add little more flour, or if is to hard add little more warm water.

Transfer dough over a flour surface place. Knead dough for 5 to 7 minutes. Transfer dough into a large floured or grease bowl. Cover and let rice for 2 hours or until double in bulk.

Punch dough down and divide in half. Shape each half into a loaf as the shape you like. Place each loaf of bread into a grease and floured pan. Cover and let rice for 1 hour. Bake at 400F. for 20 minutes, then low heat to 3 to 375 for 25 minutes.

Remove from pan and cool completely over wire rack.

Slice and serve with coffee or tea.

< Enjoy Emilia>

CUZZUPA DI PASQUA CALABRESE

Easter Bread

INGREDIENTS

½ cup milk

1 envelope dry yeast

2 ½ pounds flour

1 cup sugar

8 eggs beaten

1 tablespoon lemon zest

2 tablespoons lemon juice

½ teaspoon salt

4 boiled eggs

2 eggs beat to brush over the bread before baking

4 boiled eggs with shells for the top of the bread

DIRECTIONS

Warm the milk in a small saucepan and dissolve the dry yeast. Let stand for 5 minutes. In a large bowl add flour and make a well in the center. Add eggs, sugar, lemon zest, lemon juice and salt and work them together with your hands or a large spatula.

Add the milk mixture and mix well. Work the dough in the bowl until it is very soft, and then cover for 5 minutes. Sprinkle ½ a cup of flour on a wooden surface and work the dough for 5 minutes.

Put back into bowl, cover with a dishtowel in a warm place of your house, and put a warm blanket over the dishtowel, as that will keep dough very warm. Let rise for three hours.

Put dough back on the wooden surface with flour and divide the dough into 4 sections. Grease 4 pans of any style you like, can be a 9 x 9 round pan or 9 x 9 square pan.

Roll the dough like a snake and bring the ends together. You can make any shape you like. Press 1 boiled egg, with shell, into each Easter bread.

Take a small piece of the dough and roll thin like bucatini pasta, make a cross over the egg, press down the ends.

Cover the pan with a tablecloth and light blanket. Let rise for 1 hour, brush the Easter bread with beaten eggs, using a pastry brush to go very gently over the bread.

Bake in preheated oven at 375 F. for 10 to 15 minutes. Easter bread needs to be golden, not browned, and needs very little time to cook.

<From my family to yours. Happy Easter. Emilia>

CALZONI FRITTI DI RICOTTA E SPINACI

Fried Calzone with Ricotta Cheese, And Spinach

INGREDIENTS

4 cups all purpose flour

1 teaspoon salt

4 tablespoons olive oil

2 eggs beaten

½ cup Prosciutto diced

¾ cup Swiss cheese

1 small package frozen spinach

½ teaspoon ground black pepper

½ cup Parmesan cheese

2 eggs yolks

1 teaspoon baking powder

2 clove garlic peel and finely chopped

1 ½ cup vegetables oil to fry

DIRECTIONS

In a bowl add flour and make a well in the center. Add salt, baking pour, eggs, and 2 tablespoons oil, mix well a work the dough for 2 to 3 minutes.

Cover the bowl with a kitchen towel and let rest for 10 minutes.

Meanwhile in a skillet heath 2 remain oil and sauté garlic until golden. Sauté spinach for 1 minute or 2.

When spinach is cooling down, press the spinach threw a rice mill; this will make drying the excess oil and juice from the spinach.

When spinach are cooling down, in a small bowl mix ricotta, spinach, Parmesan cheese, eggs yolks, Prosciutto, Swiss cheese and ground black pepper.

Whisked eggs white: flatten the dough and roll very thin, cut small circles about 4 to 5 inches round.

Divide the filling into the circles: brush round circles with eggs white, and fold over. Secure the edges with fork, this will secure and give a nice decoration round the edges.

In a skillet heat oil until very hot. Cook deep fry until calzone are golden light brown. Drain well over paper towel.

If you need to make this for a party: multiplayer the recipe. You can make the filling a day ahead. This will save time if you make a large quantity.

Serve hot as appetizer, or snacks.

<Buon Appetito Emilia>

6. PASTA AND SAUCES

PASTA FUSILLI COME LI FACEVA MAMMA

My Mother's Homemade Fusilli Pasta

INGREDIENTS

4 cups semolina flour

2 tablespoons oil

1 egg

¾ cup water

DIRECTIONS

Pour flour into a large bowl and make a well in the center. Add the egg, water, a pinch salt and oil. Work mixture together and keep kneading dough until thoroughly mixed. If dough is too soft add a little flour, and if it is too dry add a little water. Turn onto a work surface and keep working the dough. It's ok to sprinkle a little flour down to keep the dough from sticking. Divide dough into small pieces, and then roll into thin logs, about the size of a 5-point knitting needle, then cut into 4-inch long pieces using a knitting needle.

Roll piece dough around a needle that has been coated with a little oil and gently roll until you have the curly shape of fusilli pasta. Slide curls onto a tablecloth or dishtowel that has been lightly sprinkled with flour and cover until it is time to cook. Cook pasta in a large pot of salted boiling water. When pasta floats to the top, drain and rinse with cool water. (Homemade pasta has a lot of starch.)

Top with your favorite sauce and serve hot.

You can also freeze the pasta at this stage. Just lay fusilli on a flat tray with a layer of waxed paper separating layers of pasta.

<From my Mother to me, and now to you. Enjoy! Emilia>

SALSA CASALINGA PER LA CONSERVA

Preserved Canned Tomatoes

INGREDIENTS

26 pounds of Roma tomatoes

8 Mason jars, 1 pint

1 extra large saucepot, 25 quarts

8 teaspoons salt

DIRECTIONS

Wash tomatoes in water, remove the core and cut in half. In the saucepan add one quart or water and bring to a boil. Fill the pot with cut tomatoes, leaving 3 inches of room at the top. Keep stirring every so often with a large wooden spatula, or the tomatoes will burn to the bottom of pan. Boil until tomatoes are soft, which will take about 10 minutes. Drain and let cool down before starting to grind. You may have to boil the tomatoes in two batches.

I wash my jars and lids in the dishwasher, buy you can sterilize them in a big saucepot with boiling water. Let jars drain and lids dry.

Use electric tomato grinder or a food mill to process the tomatoes and pour all the sauce into a big saucepan or plastic container. Add about 4 to 5 tablespoons of salt, mix thoroughly and start to fill the jars, leaving ½ inch of room at the top of the jar. Wipe rims and lids, screw down lids and bands. Fill a large pot with hot water, as this will speed the time to boil. Also remember that the water will need to be 2 inches above the tops of jars once they are immersed in the water. Use tongs to gently place jars into the boiling water and add additional hot water as you go along if needed.

Bring to a boil again, cover the pan and let boil for 20 minutes. Leave cover on until water is cool. When jars and water are cool, take jars of saucepan and dry with paper towel or kitchen towel. Put jars in the coolest place in the house. These can be used and saved over the course of 1 year.

To make fresh sauce, use the jars of tomato sauce as the base for the spices and other ingredients you want to add. Or right after grinding the tomatoes, heat olive oil, about 2 tablespoon per jar, and add the spices you like in your sauce. Add ½ cup of water per jar, bring to a boil and cook on low heat for 30 minutes. Then use the canning process above, but be sure to mark the jars as "sauce" so you don't forget and think that they are just plain tomatoes!

<Have fun! With your family. Emilia>

SALSA SEMPLICE AL POMODORO

Simple Tomato Sauce

INGREDIENTS

½ cup extra virgin olive oil

1 small onion, finely chopped

½ cup prosciutto, diced

1 can (28 oz.) tomatoes, peeled

3 basil leaves

¼ teaspoon fresh ground pepper

1 pinch salt to taste

DIRECTIONS

In a large skillet, heat oil and sauté onion until light golden, then add prosciutto and sauté until light brown. Add tomatoes and spices to the skillet and bring to a boil. Reduce heat and simmer, partially covered with the lid, for about 25 minutes.

If fresh basil leaves are out season, you can substitute ½ teaspoon dried basil flakes.

Serve over your favorite pasta or pizza.

<Enjoy! Emilia>

SALSA ALL'ARRABIATA

Fresh Spicy Tomato Sauce

INGREDIENTS

2 tablespoons extra virgin olive oil

2 cloves of garlic, crushed

2 anchovy fillets, chopped

2 pounds fresh tomatoes, peeled and diced

¼ cup fresh basil, chopped

2 hot red chili peppers, seeds removed and chopped

1 pinch salt and red pepper

3 oz. black olives

DIRECTIONS

In a large skillet, heat the oil and sauté the garlic. When garlic is golden add the anchovies. Stir in the tomatoes with the juice, and then add the basil, chili peppers, salt and pepper. Bring to a boil, reduce heat, and simmer partially covered for 20 minutes. Then add ¼ cup water and the olives and cook for 10 minutes.

Serve over your favorite cooked pasta.

<Have fun! In the kitchen! Emilia>

SALSA ALLA MARINARA

Marinara Sauce

INGREDIENTS

2 tablespoons extra virgin olive oil

4 cloves of garlic, crushed

2 tablespoons onion, chopped

¼ teaspoon salt

¼ teaspoon red pepper flakes

1 tablespoon fresh basil leaves, chopped

1 can (28 oz.) diced tomatoes

DIRECTIONS

In a large skillet, heat the oil and sauté the garlic and onions until golden. Stir in the tomatoes with their juices and add the remaining ingredients. Bring to a boil, reduce heat and simmer partially covered for 20 minutes. Then add ¼ cup water, cover and cook for at least 10 more minutes.

Serve over your favorite cooked pasta.

<Enjoy! Emilia>

SALSA CON LE MALANZANE

Eggplant Sauce

INGREDIENTS

¼ cup extra virgin olive oil

4 cloves of garlic, crushed

½ cup onions, sliced

1 can (14 oz.) crushed tomatoes

6 baby eggplants, chopped

½ cup fresh basil leaves, chopped

½ cup fresh parsley, chopped

1 pinch salt and ground pepper to taste

1 cup button white mushrooms, sliced

DIRECTIONS

In a large skillet, heat the oil and sauté the garlic and onions until golden. Add crushed tomatoes and bring to a boil. Cook for 5 minutes, and then add eggplant and spices. Reduce heat and simmer for 2 minutes. (Remember that this type of vegetable will cook very fast.) Stir in mushrooms and simmer for 5 more minutes.

Serve over your favorite pasta or pizza.

<Eat well. Emilia>

SALSA ALLA PUTTANESCA DI CALABRIA

Calabrian Puttanesca Sauce

INGREDIENTS

3 tablespoons extra virgin olive oil

4 cloves of garlic, peeled and chopped

2 tablespoons onion, minced

1 pound grape tomatoes, cut in half and seeded

2 hot red chili peppers, seeds removed and chopped

¼ teaspoon fresh ground black pepper

¼ cup dry white wine

½ cup thinly sliced black olives

¼ cup capers, preserved in oil and chopped

¼ cup fresh parsley, chopped

¼ cup fresh basil leaves, chopped

DIRECTIONS

Heat oil in a medium saucepan. Add garlic and sauté until golden, then add onion and sauté until softened. Add tomatoes and cook on low heat, partially covered, for 10 minutes. Add remaining ingredients and simmer for 5 minutes.

If you can't get fresh chill peppers, add 1 teaspoon hot red pepper flakes. This will add the same spice. Pour sauce over a dish of spaghetti pasta.

<Buon Appetito! Emilia>

EMILIA PASTA AL FORNO

Emilia's Baked Ziti

INGREDIENTS

For the Meatballs:

8 oz. ground beef

1/4 cup Romano cheese, grated

¼ teaspoon salt

2 eggs

1 teaspoon fresh parsley, chopped

1/4 cup vegetable oil

For the Pasta:

1 pound (16oz. dried) ziti

6 cups marinara sauce

8 oz. mozzarella, sliced

¼ teaspoon salt

¼ teaspoon black pepper

½ cup Romano cheese, grated

4 fresh basil leaves

2 boiled eggs, sliced

DIRECTIONS

Preheat oven to 350 F.

Meatballs! Mix ground beef, ¼ cup grated Romano, parsley, 1/2 the salt, the eggs and the parsley in a large bowl. Thoroughly mix all ingredients and shape meat into bite size shapes, as small as chickpeas. In a large non-stick pan, heat oil and cook the meatballs for 2 minutes, stir them once, then use a spatula to transfer the meatballs from the pan to a plate covered with paper towels.

Cook the ziti according to package directions and drain. Transfer pasta into a mix bowl: add 2 cups of the marinara sauce and ¼ cup of Romano cheese: gently mix to coat pasta and sauce.

Then in a large baking pan, put 1 cup of the marinara sauce on the bottom and spread half of the pasta over the sauce. Then add 1/4 cup of the Romano cheese, the meatballs and the 2 sliced eggs. Cover with 1 cup sauce and add the remaining pasta and then the remaining Romano cheese.

Top with sliced mozzarella and bake in at for about 25 minutes, or until mozzarella cheese is melted and pasta is lightly golden brown.

Serve pasta hot from the oven.

<Buon Appetito! Emilia>

SALSA AL PESTO

Pesto Sauce

INGREDIENTS

4 cups fresh basil

6 cloves of garlic, peeled

1 ½ cups extra virgin olive oil

½ teaspoon salt

½ teaspoon black pepper

2 cups fresh Italian parsley

1 cup pine nuts

DIRECTIONS

In a food processor, place the basil leaves, parsley, pine nuts, garlic, salt and pepper. Cover and process until finely chopped. Add oil, cover and process for 5 minutes until the mixture is pureed.

Pesto can be frozen, for whenever you need it, up to 5 to 6 months, or it can be refrigerated up to 3 or 4 weeks.

Serve over your favorite pasta.

If you have small garden, take advantage. Plant basil and use to make your marinara and pesto sauces.

<This can be fun! Emilia>

LINGUINE AL SUGO CON ZUCCHINI

Linguine with Zucchini Sauce

INGREDIENTS

4 pounds Italian zucchini

4 cloves of garlic, peeled and thinly sliced

1 small onion, finely chopped

½ teaspoon salt and ground black pepper

½ cup fresh basil leaves, chopped thinly

¼ cup fresh parsley, chopped

½ cup white wine

½ cup Parmesan cheese, grated

1 lb. (16 oz. dried) linguine

DIRECTIONS

Wash and cut zucchini lengthwise, scoop out the white portion of the zucchini with a spoon and slice 1 ½ inch long by ½ inch wide. Heat oil in a large pan and add zucchini, garlic, onion, salt and black pepper, then add half the basil leaves and half the parsley. Stir and sauté zucchini mixture for 2 minutes. Add wine and cook for 5 minutes, or until zucchini are tender.

Cook pasta according to package directions, drain and toss with zucchini mixture in the pan over medium heat. And add half of the Parmesan. Transfer pasta to a serving platter and top with the remaining Parmesan, basil and parsley.

Serve when the pasta is hot.

<Buon Appetito! Emilia>

FETTUCCINE ALFREDO

Fettuccini Alfredo

INGREDIENTS

1 lb. (16 oz. dried) fettuccine pasta

½ teaspoon black pepper

1 cup heavy cream

½ cup Parmesan cheese

1 tablespoon fresh parsley, chopped

DIRECTIONS

Melt butter in a large saucepan. Add the cream and bring to a boil. Reduce heat and simmer for 5 minutes, then add half of the Parmesan cheese and add salt and pepper to taste. Turn off the heat until fettuccine is finished cooking.

Cook pasta according to package directions, drain and add to the Alfredo saucepan. Turn on the heat, toss well to combine ingredients and heat throughout, and season to taste.

Transfer fettuccini to a serving dish and sprinkle with the remaining cheese and fresh chopped parsley. Serve hot.

<Eat well, Emilia>

LINGUINI PASTA CON PESCE AL SUGO DI LIMONE

Lemon Seafood Linguine

INGREDIENTS

1 lb. scallops

2 lb. mussels

¾ cup white wine

1 ¼ cup water

1 tablespoon lemon zest

1 tablespoon olive oil

1 tablespoon butter

4 cloves of garlic, crushed

½ cup red onions, chopped

10 oz. linguine pasta

1 tablespoon lemon juice

1 tablespoons fresh or dried oregano

½ teaspoon black pepper

1 tablespoon fresh Italian parsley

DIRECTIONS

Scrub mussels remove beards. Combine mussels, water and ½ cup wine in a pan. Cover, bring to a boil and simmer until mussels are open. Strain mussels, and reserving the liquid. Add the lemon zest to strained liquid and simmer for 5 minutes.

Cook pasta according to package directions and drain.

In a large nonstick skillet add oil, butter, garlic, onions and sauté until golden and brown. Add scallops, oregano, black pepper, and lemon juice, remaining ¼ cup of white wine and 1 cup of the strained liquid. Simmer for 5 minutes, add linguine pasta and toss well.

Transfer pasta to a large dish and top with fresh parsley. Serve hot.

<This is a Calabrian-style dish. Enjoy! Emilia>

FETTUCCINI DI SPINACI CON PEPERONI- ROSSI &VERDI

Spinach Fettuccini with Red and Green Peppers

INGREDIENTS

8 oz. spinach fettuccine pasta

2 tablespoons olive oil

2 cloves of garlic, peeled and chopped

1 tablespoon onions, chopped

3 skinless boneless chicken breasts

½ teaspoon black pepper

¼ teaspoon salt

1 large green bell pepper, thinly sliced

1 large red bell pepper, thinly sliced

½ cup dry white wine

½ cup water

1 tablespoon cornstarch

DIRECTIONS

In a large sauté pan add garlic and onions. Stir until golden, and then cut chicken into thin strips and add to the pan along with salt and black pepper. Stir for 5 more minutes.

Add green and red peppers, toss for 3 minutes, then and add wine, water, and cornstarch. Stir over heat until sauce boils and thickens.

Cook pasta according to package directions, drain and add to the chicken mixture.

Serve when pasta is hot.

<This is my favorite pasta dish. Emilia>

Emilia Fusco

PENNE CON SALSA E CARNE MACINATA PICCANTE

Spiced Penne With Meat Sauce

INGREDIENTS

1 lb. penne pasta

3 oz ground beef

3 oz ground lean pork

2 tablespoons olive oil

2 cloves of garlic, peeled and crushed

½ cup red onions, chopped

3 chili pepper chopped

1 cup button mushrooms, sliced

½ teaspoon black pepper

½ teaspoon salt

½ teaspoon oregano, fresh or dried

1 28 oz can tomatoes peel

½ cup water

2 tablespoons fresh basil, thinly sliced

2 tablespoons fresh parsley, chopped

½ cup Parmesan cheese, grated

DIRECTIONS

In a large nonstick pan heat oil and sauté garlic and onions until golden brown. Add ground meats and sauté until meats is no longer pink. Add tomatoe peels, chili pepper, mushrooms, salt, black pepper, and oregano, and basil leaves.

Cook and stir for 5 minutes, then add ½ water, cover and simmer for 5 minutes.

Cook pasta according to package directions, drain and transfer to a serving dish. Pour all of the vegetables over the penne and add ¼ cup grated cheese. Gently mix and garnish the pasta with the remaining Parmesan cheese.

Serve when pasta is hot.

<Buon Appetito Emilia>

EMILIA PASTA PRIMAVERA

Calabrian Penne Primavera

INGREDIENTS

1 pound (16 oz.) dried fettuccine pasta

2 tablespoons extra virgin olive oil

3 cloves of garlic, peeled and chopped

1 cup tomatoes, peeled and chopped

2 tablespoons fresh basil leaves, chopped

½ cup zucchini, cut into 1-inch pieces

½ cup green bell pepper, cut into 1-inch pieces

½ cup broccoli florets

½ cup button mushroom slices

¼ cup celery, chopped

½ teaspoon salt and pepper

1 pinch salt and black pepper

¼ cup Parmesan cheese, grated

DIRECTIONS

Heat oil in a large skillet and sauté garlic until golden and brown. Add tomatoes and sauté for 5 minutes, then add all the ingredients above and simmer for 10 minutes.

Cook pasta according to package directions, drain and add to the vegetable mixture and toss well.

Transfer pasta to serving dish and sprinkle with the grated Parmesan. Serve when pasta is very hot.

Makes 6 servings.

<Enjoy! Emilia>

LINGUINE ALLE VONGOLE DI CALABRIA

Calabrian Spicy Clam Linguini

INGREDIENTS

1 pound (16 oz. dried) linguine

2 tablespoons extra virgin olive oil

1 tablespoon butter

4 cloves of garlic, peeled and chopped

1 can (15 oz.) clams do not drain juices

1 pinch salt

¼ teaspoon black pepper

1 hot red chili pepper, seeds removed and chopped

½ cup white dry wine

DIRECTIONS

In a large skillet, heat oil and butter and sauté garlic until golden brown. Add clams with the juices, salt, black pepper, chopped chili pepper and wine. Simmer for 5 minutes.

Cook pasta according to package directions, drain and add to the skillet with the clams. Simmer for 30 seconds.

Transfer linguine to a serving dish and sprinkle with chopped parsley. Serve when pasta is hot.

Remember when cooking pasta and fish or seafood together, never add cheese over the pasta.

Makes 6 servings.

<Buon Appetito! Emilia>

LINGUINE PASTA CON PORCHETTA, AGLIO A OLIO

Linguini with Italian Pancetta, Garlic and Oil

INGREDIENTS

10 oz. linguine pasta

6 oz. Italian pancetta

4 cloves of garlic, peeled and minced

¼ cup extra virgin olive oil

1 teaspoon oregano flakes

2 tablespoons fresh basil leaves, chopped

DIRECTIONS

In a small bowl mix oil and garlic to blend well, then heat garlic and oil and sauté until golden brown. Add pancetta and oregano to the pan, sauté for 2 minutes and set aside.

Cook linguine pasta according to package directions, drain and toss with the pancetta, garlic and oil. Serve on a platter topped with chopped fresh basil.

Make 6 servings.

<Enjoy! Emilia>

TORTELLINI CON PROSCIUTTO A PEZZETTI

Prosciutto Tortellini

INGREDIENTS

1 pound (16 oz. dried) cheese tortellini

2 oz. butter

1 tablespoon flour

1 cup heavy cream

4 oz. prosciutto Parma, julienne sliced

¾ cup frozen sweet peas (defrosted)

½ cup grated Parmesan cheese

DIRECTIONS

Preheat oven to 350 F.

Cook tortellini according to the package directions, drain well and set aside.

Melt butter in a small saucepan, stir in the flour, and then add the heavy cream. Bring to a light boil, reduce heat and simmer until the mixture is light yellow. Add julienne prosciutto and defrosted sweet peas to the cream mixture and turn off the heat.

Butter a large baking dish. Spread tortellini in baking dish and cover with cream mixture. Sprinkle with Parmesan cheese and cover with three slices of prosciutto. Bake for 25 minutes.

Makes 4 servings.

<Enjoy! Emilia>

PANCETTA FETTUCCINE

Fettuccine Carbonara

INGREDIENTS

10 oz. fettuccine pasta

6 oz. pancetta, diced

½ cup sour cream

¼ teaspoon black pepper

2 cloves of garlic, peeled and minced

½ cup Parmesan cheese, grated

½ cup fresh Italian parsley, finely chopped

DIRECTIONS

Cook fettuccine according to the package directions, drain well and set aside.

While the fettuccine is boiling, cook pancetta in a large skillet over medium heat until crisp. Pour off and discard the fat and remove skillet from heat.

Beat sour cream, pepper and garlic together in a medium bowl and set aside. Return pancetta skillet to the stove on medium heat. Stir in Parmesan cheese and parsley. Add fettuccine to the skillet and toss until well coated and hot. Add sour cream mixture, tossing pasta until evenly coated. Serve hot.

Makes 6 servings

<Buon Appetito! Emilia>

CALABRESE LINGUNI PASTA E ARROSTO DI MAIALE

Southern Italian Linguini with Pork Tenderloin

INGREDIENTS

8 oz. linguine pasta

½ pound pork tenderloin

2 tablespoons olive oil

4 cloves of garlic, peeled and chopped

¼ cup onion, minced

1 cup piccante (spicy) Italian sauce

¾ cup frozen peas

¾ cup red sweet pepper, cut into 1-inch strips

½ teaspoon dry oregano flakes

½ cup Italian parsley, chopped

½ teaspoon salt

½ teaspoon ground black pepper

DIRECTIONS

Trim any fat off of the pork, cut into thin bite size strips and set aside.

In a large skillet add oil, chopped garlic and onions and sauté over medium heat until golden brown. Add meat to the skillet and cook for four minutes until meat is browned.

Add piccante sauce, frozen peas, red bell pepper, oregano, half the parsley, black pepper, and salt. Cook uncovered for 5 minutes.

Cook linguine pasta in lightly salted boiling water according to package directions, drain and add linguine to the skillet. Toss to coat with sauce. Transfer pasta to a large serving dish and garnish with remaining parsley and some grated Romano cheese.

Makes 6 servings.

<Buon Appetito! Emilia>

EMILIA'S PENNE CON SALSICCIE E PEPERONI BRUCENTI

Emilia's Penne with Sausage & Hot Peppers

INGREDIENTS

12 oz. penne pasta

2 tablespoon extra virgin olive oil

4 cloves of garlic, peeled and crushed

1 pound hot Italian sausage

1 cup Italian plum tomatoes, seeded and chopped

4 basil leaves

¼ cup water

½ cup green bell pepper cut in 1-inch strips

½ cup red sweet pepper cut in 1-inch strips

2 jalapeño peppers, seeded and chopped

1 teaspoon salt

½ teaspoon ground black pepper

½ cup parsley, chopped

½ cup Romano cheese, grated

DIRECTIONS

Cut sausage into ¾ inch rings. In large skillet heat oil, add garlic and sauté until golden brown. Add sausage and cook for four minutes on medium heat. Add tomatoes, basil leaves, water, chopped bell peppers, jalapeño peppers, salt and pepper. Let simmer for 10 minutes, partially covered, on low heat.

Cook pasta in lightly salted boiling water according to package directions, drain and pour pasta into skillet. Add half of the cheese, half of the chopped parsley and toss gently. Transfer pasta to a serving platter and garnish with remaining Romano cheese and parsley.

Serve hot.

Makes 6 servings.

<Buon Appetito! Emilia>

SPAGHETTI A QUATTRO FORMAGGI

Four Cheese Spaghetti

INGREDIENTS

8 oz. spaghetti pasta

1 package frozen mixed vegetables

¼ cup low fat milk

½ cup fontina cheese, shredded

½ cup provolone cheese, shredded

¼ cup Romano cheese, grated

¼ cup Parmesan cheese, grated

DIRECTIONS

In large saucepan cook spaghetti pasta according to the package directions, but add the frozen vegetables in last two minutes of cooking time. Drain spaghetti and vegetables when al dente. Return spaghetti and vegetables in the saucepan add fontina cheese, milk, provolone, and Romano cheeses. To

Toss spaghetti and transfer spaghetti mixture and to a large serving platter, and sprinkle with the Parmesan. Serve hot.

Makes 4 servings.

<Enjoy! Emilia>

SALSA ALLA SICILIANA

Sicilian Tomato Sauce

INGREDIENTS

½ cup pine nuts

¼ cup extra virgin olive oil

¼ teaspoon ground pepper

½ teaspoon salt

2 cloves of garlic, peeled and chopped

2 cups fresh basil leaves, chopped

2 pounds fresh Italian plum tomatoes, seeded and quartered

2 tablespoons Parmesan cheese

DIRECTIONS

In a food processor combine pine nuts, oil, salt, pepper, garlic and one cup of the basil leaves. Pulse one or two times until the pine nuts are chopped.

Add half the tomatoes and process for 30 second. Add tomatoes, remaining basil leaves and Parmesan cheese. Mix with a wooden spoon and serve over your favorite pasta.

This can be refrigerated for 3 days, or it will freeze well for up to 1 month.

<Have fun! Emilia>

FETTUCCINE CON GAMBERI E SPINACI

Fettuccini with Shrimp & Spinach

INGREDIENTS

8 oz. dry spinach fettuccine pasta

2 tablespoons extra virgin olive oil

2 cloves of garlic, peeled and chopped

½ cup onions, sliced

2 cups plum tomatoes, peeled, seeded and chopped

½ teaspoon dried oregano flakes

¼ teaspoon dried tarragon

1 pound (frozen) shrimp, peeled and divined

¼ cup fresh parsley, chopped

½ cup Parmesan cheese, grated

DIRECTIONS

Sauté oil, garlic and onions in a large skillet until golden, and then add tomatoes, basil, tarragon salt and black pepper. Cook for 10 minutes on low to medium heat. Add shrimp and cook until pink.

Cook pasta in lightly salted boiling water according to package directions, drain, pour pasta into skillet with the shrimp and toss gently. Transfer pasta to a serving platter and garnish with the Parmesan and parsley. Serve hot.

Makes 4 serving.

<Buon Appetito! Emilia>

LINGUINE PASTA ALL`AROME DI BASILICO

Tomato Linguini with Basil

INGREDIENTS

¼ cup extra virgin olive oil

4 cloves of garlic, peeled and chopped

2 pounds fresh plum tomatoes, seeded and chopped

¼ teaspoon ground black pepper

1 teaspoon salt

¾ cup fresh basil leaves, chopped into halves

¼ cup Parmesan cheese, grated

DIRECTIONS

Heat oil in a large skillet and sauté garlic until golden. Add tomatoes, half the salt and black pepper, and half the basil leaves. Cook at a low simmer for 5 minutes, and then add a ¼ cup of water and simmer for an additional 10 minutes.

Cook pasta in lightly salted boiling water according to package directions, drain, and pour pasta into a serving bowl. Top with the tomato sauce and half of the Parmesan. Toss gently. Garnish linguini with remaining cheese and basil leaves.

Makes 6 servings.

<Buon Appetito! Emilia>

PASTA CON CARNE DI MANZO

Beef & Penne Pasta

INGREDIENTS

1 pound (16 oz. dried) penne pasta

1 pound beef tenderloin, cut in 2 inch strips

1 tablespoon all-purpose flour

4 cloves of garlic, peeled and minced

½ cup onion, minced

2 cups tomatoes, seeded and chopped

2 tablespoons extra virgin olive oil

1 zucchini (cut lengthwise and seeded) cut into 1 inch strips

1 can (15 oz.) sliced mushrooms

½ teaspoon ground black pepper

1 teaspoon salt

¼ teaspoon dried oregano flakes

¼ cup fresh basil leaves, torn for garnish

DIRECTIONS

Heat oil in a large skillet and sauté beef until no long pink. Add flour, garlic and onion and sauté until golden, then add all vegetables and seasonings to the skillet. Stir until vegetables are tender. Add ¼ cup of water if needed. Cook on low heat until the sauce is thick.

Cook pasta in lightly salted boiling water according to package directions, drain, and pour pasta into a serving bowl. Spoon beef mixture over the pasta, garnish with torn basil and 2 tablespoons of grated Parmesan cheese.

181

Makes 6 servings.

<Have fun! Emilia>

PESCE ASSORTITE ALLA PROVINCIALE

Seafood Provincial

INGREDIENTS

1 pound (16 oz. dried) egg fettuccine

1 ½ cups water

2 cups dry white wine

1 lemon, thinly sliced

4 cloves of garlic, peeled and chopped

1 ½ pound shrimp, shelled & tails left on

1 ½ mussels, beards removed and well scrubbed

1 ½ pound halibut, cut into 1-½ inch cubes

2 tablespoons butter

2 tablespoons oil

2 tablespoons all-purpose flour

¾ cup cream

½ cup Italian parsley, chopped

DIRECTIONS

In a large saucepan bring water, wine, sliced lemon and chopped garlic to a boil. Add halibut and cook for four minutes. Remove to a platter and set aside. Add shrimp to the pan and cook for 3 minutes, then remove and set aside. Finally, add mussels to the pan and remove when the shells open. Strain wine mixture through fine cheesecloth.

Melt butter and flour in a small saucepan, then whisk in the wine mixture. Bring to simmer and then stir in the cream, salt and black pepper to taste. Cook until the mixture comes to a boil and thickens.

Cook pasta in lightly salted boiling water according to package directions, drain, pour pasta into a serving platter and arrange the mussels around the edge. Gently mix halibut and shrimp into sauce and pour over the fettuccini. Garnish with chopped parsley.

Serve with a mixed salad and sesame Italian bread sticks.

Makes 6 servings.

<Buon Appetito! Emilia>

ORECCHIETTE CAPRICCIOSE

Crazy Orecchiette Pasta

INGREDIENTS

12 oz. orecchiette pasta

1 tablespoon butter

2 tablespoons extra virgin olive oil

2 cloves of garlic, peeled and chopped

½ cup white onion, minced

4 oz. sausage

1 stalk of celery, chopped

1 carrot, chopped

1 (28 oz.) cans whole peeled tomatoes

1 hot red chili pepper, chopped

½ teaspoon salt

¼ teaspoon ground black pepper

½ cup Romano cheese, grated

1 tablespoon parsley, chopped

2 tablespoons fresh basil, chopped

DIRECTIONS

In a large skillet, heat butter and oil and sauté garlic until golden, then add onion, sausage, celery, carrot, chili pepper, salt and pepper. Simmer at low heat until meat is browned. Add tomatoes, using a fork or your hand to crush the tomatoes. Simmer for 20 minutes, adding ½ cup water if need.

185

Cook pasta in lightly salted boiling water according to package directions, drain, and pour pasta into a serving platter. Pour sauce over the pasta, add half the Romano cheese and toss gently. Garnish with remaining Romano and chopped parsley and basil. Serve hot.

Makes 6 servings.

<Buon Appetito! Emilia>

PENNE CON VEGETALE PICCANTE

Penne with Spicy Vegetables

INGREDIENTS

1 pound (16 oz. dried) penne rigate

2 oz. pancetta, cut into cubes

1 tablespoon extra virgin olive oil

3 cloves of garlic, peeled and chopped

1 pound cherry tomatoes, cut in half

2 cups zucchini cut lengthwise, and chopped to the same size as the penne

1 tablespoon sage, chopped fine

½ tablespoon rosemary flakes

4 basil leaves, shredded

2 hot cherry peppers, seeds removed and chopped

2 tablespoons fresh parsley, chopped

DIRECTIONS

In a nonstick saucepan, sauté pancetta until golden and brown. Drain fat from the pan and transfer pancetta to a plate covered with paper towels. Add oil to the pan and sauté garlic until golden, then add tomatoes and simmer for 10 minutes, add all the remaining ingredients, except the parsley, and cook for 10 minutes.

Cook pasta in lightly salted boiling water according to package directions, drain, and pour pasta into the tomato sauce. Sauté for 30 seconds and transfer to a serving platter. Garnish with Romano cheese and fresh parsley. Serve hot.

Makes 6 servings.

<From my kitchen to your table. Buon Appetito! Emilia>

PASTA ALLA CALABRESE

Southern Italian Pasta

INGREDIENTS

5 sardines

2 tablespoons extra virgin olive oil

4 cloves of garlic, peeled and chopped

½ cup capers, packed in oil

1 pound (16 oz. dry) bucatini

¾ cup black olives, pitted

½ teaspoon ground black pepper

¼ teaspoon salt

2 oz. stale bread

DIRECTIONS

Wash sardines with running water to remove the salt and chop into pieces. In a frying pan heat the oil and sauté garlic until golden. Add chopped sardines, capers, olives, salt and pepper and cook well.

Cook pasta in lightly salted boiling water according to package directions. Just before pasta is finished, add the stale bread to the pan containing the oil mixture in crumbs, or alternatively toast lightly as cubes and then add to the oil. Mix together until the bread has a golden color.

Drain pasta, place in a bowl, pour oil and sardine mixture over and toss gently. Serve hot. No cheese is needed for this dish.

Makes 4 servings.

<Have fun! Emilia>

SPAGHETTI ALLE VONGOLE

Spaghetti with Clams

INGREDIENTS

2 pounds clams

1 pound (16 oz. dry) spaghetti

2 tablespoons extra virgin olive oil

2 cloves of garlic, peeled and chopped

1 cup tomatoes, peeled and chopped

2 tablespoons fresh basil leaves, chopped

½ teaspoon red hot-pepper flakes

½ teaspoon black pepper

¼ teaspoon salt

2 tablespoons fresh parsley, chopped

DIRECTIONS

Wash the clams in a high-sided casserole dish and drain the liquid. Place on low heat and allow the clams to open, and then remove the fleshy meat from inside. Drain the juice and save for later.

In a frying pan, add oil and garlic and sauté until golden, then add tomatoes and simmer for 5 minutes on high heat. Add clam juice and simmer for 5 more minutes. Add chopped basil leaves, salt, red pepper and black pepper. Add clams and cook for another 2 minutes on low heat.

Cook pasta in lightly salted boiling water according to package directions, drain, and pour pasta into a serving bowl. Top with clam sauce, toss and garnish with chopped parsley. Serve hot.

Makes 5 servings.

<Buon Appetito! Emilia>

FETTUCCINI ALLE SPINACE E AL PEPERONCINO

Spicy Spinach Fettuccini

INGREDIENTS

6 medium skinless boneless chicken breasts

1 pound (16 oz.) dry spinach fettuccini

½ teaspoon salt

½ teaspoon ground black pepper

1 teaspoon fresh ginger, chopped

2 cloves of garlic, peeled and chopped

½ cup olive oil

1 cup onion, sliced

1 cup tomatoes, peeled chopped

1 hot red chili pepper, chopped

¼ cup Parmesan cheese, grated

DIRECTIONS

Combine salt, black pepper, ginger, and half of the chopped garlic. Rub the mixture over the chicken. In skillet heat oil, sauté rest of garlic and onions until golden. Add chicken to the skillet and cook on low heat for 5 minutes or until chicken is no longer pink. Remove chicken from skillet and slice crosswise into strips.

Add tomatoes and chili pepper and simmer for 10 minutes, then return chicken to the skillet and cook for an additional 10 minutes.

Cook pasta in lightly salted boiling water according to package directions, drain, and pour pasta into the skillet. Add grated cheese and transfer pasta to a serving platter. Serve hot.

Makes 6 servings.

<Buon Appetito! Emilia>

PASTA CALABRESE AGLIO E OLIO

Calabrese-style Pasta with Garlic & Oil

INGREDIENTS

1 pound (16 oz.) bucatini pasta

3 tablespoons extra virgin olive oil

4 clove garlic, peeled and chopped

6 anchovy fillets, washed and chopped

¼ teaspoon black pepper

1 small hot red chili pepper, chopped

½ cup plain breadcrumbs

DIRECTIONS

Cook pasta in lightly salted boiling water according to package directions.

Meanwhile, heat oil in a skillet, add garlic and sauté until golden. Add anchovies, black pepper, and chili pepper and sauté for 1 minute on low heat. Drain pasta al dente and transfer to a serving platter.

Top with anchovy sauce and breadcrumbs. Toss gently and serve hot.

Makes 4 servings.

<Enjoy! Emilia>

SPAGHETTI AL TONNO

Tuna & Spaghetti

INGREDIENTS

1 pound (16 oz. dry) thin spaghetti

1 tablespoon olive oil

2 cloves of garlic, peeled and chopped

1 can (28 oz.) whole peeled tomatoes

½ teaspoon salt

½ teaspoon ground black pepper

4 basil leaves, chopped

1 can (6 oz.) chunk tuna packed in water, drained

¼ cup parsley, chopped

DIRECTIONS

In a skillet, sauté garlic until golden, then add tomatoes and crush with a fork. Add salt, pepper and basil leaves. Let cook for 20 minutes on medium heat, then add ¼ cup water and the add tuna. Let simmer for 10 minutes more, or until the sauce has a rich and thick consistency.

Cook pasta in lightly salted boiling water according to package directions, drain, and pour pasta into a serving bowl. Add tuna sauce and toss gently. Garnish with chopped parsley and serve hot.

Makes 4 servings.

<Buon Appetito! Emilia>

BUCATINI PASTA ALLA MATRICIANA

Matriciana Pasta

INGREDIENTS

1 pound bucatini

½ cup extra virgin olive oil

2 oz. pancetta or (guanciale) cut in small piece

2 cloves of garlic, peeled and chopped

1 medium yellow onion, minced

1 can (28 oz.) crushed tomatoes

¼ cup Romano cheese, grated

¼ cup Parmesan cheese, grated

½ teaspoon salt

2 small hot red peppers, seeded and chopped

DIRECTIONS

In a skillet heat 2 tablespoons oil and sauté pancetta until golden brown. Transfer to a plate covered with paper towels and set aside. Drain excess oil from skillet and add remaining olive oil, heat and sauté garlic until golden. Add onions, sauté until golden, then tomatoes and chili peppers and cook for 15 minutes on medium heat, stirring occasionally.

Cook pasta in lightly salted boiling water according to package directions, drain, and pour pasta into the skillet. Add half the Romano, half the Parmesan, then toss and cook for 1 minute. Transfer to a serving platter and sprinkle with remaining cheese. Serve hot.

Makes 4 servings.

<Buon Appetito! Emilia>

PASTA GEMELLI CON INSALATA CAPRESE

Gemelli with Caprice Salad Topping

INGREDIENTS

1 pound gemelli pasta

2 tablespoons extra virgin olive oil

1 tablespoon butter

1 cup fresh basil leaves, chopped

1 teaspoon salt

2 cloves of garlic, peeled and chopped

2 large tomatoes, thinly sliced and quartered

2 large buffalo mozzarella rounds, cut into 1 inch strips

1 tablespoon balsamic vinegar

1 teaspoon oregano flakes

DIRECTIONS

Cook pasta in lightly salted boiling water according to package directions, drain, and return pasta to the pan. Mix in the olive oil and butter and cover to keep warm.

Meanwhile, add half the basil, salt and garlic to a blender and mix until you have a paste.

Put tomatoes and mozzarella slices in a small bowl and pour the balsamic vinegar over them. Toss gently.

Transfer pasta to a large serving platter, top with the mixture from the blender, toss and then add the tomato/mozzarella mix. Garnish with remaining chopped basil leaves.

Makes 6 servings.

<Buon Appetito! Emilia>

SALSA TONNATA

Tuna Sauce

INGREDIENTS

½ cup yellow onion, minced

½ cup celery cut in ½ inch pieces

2 anchovy filets packed in oil, chopped

1 cup dry white wine

4 oz. tuna packed in water, drained

2 tablespoons mayonnaise

¼ teaspoon salt

¼ teaspoon ground black pepper

DIRECTIONS

In a saucepan add onion, celery and anchovies. Stir on low heat for 1 minute. Add wine, stir and cover.

Cook at a low simmer for 20 minutes, and then transfer sauce to an electric blender and process until the sauce turns into a cream. Transfer into a bowl, and then add tuna, mayonnaise, salt and black pepper. Gently stir thoroughly. You can store sauce in the refrigerator for 2 days. Serve with your favorite meats or fish.

<Have fun! Emilia>

PASTA CARA MIA ALLA OLIVE

Pasta with Black Olives

INGREDIENTS

1 pound penne pasta

2 cups marinara sauce

¾ cup fresh mozzarella cheese, cut into small pieces

5 oz. pitted black olives

¼ cup Parmesan cheese, grated

DIRECTIONS

Preheat oven to 350 F.

Cook pasta in lightly salted boiling water according to package directions, drain, and set aside.

In the meantime heat the marinara sauce, and then mix sauce and pasta in a baking dish. Add cubed mozzarella cheese, black olives and toss gently. Bake for four minutes, and then remove from the oven and sprinkle with the Parmesan cheese. Serve hot.

I named this dish after my granddaughter, Cara Mia, because she loves black olives!

Makes 6 servings

<From Cara Mia and I. Buon Appetito! Emilia>

SPAGHETTI ALLA CIOCIARA

Center of Italy Spaghetti

INGREDIENTS

1 pound spaghetti

¼ cup olive oil

2 cloves of garlic, peeled and chopped

1 can (28 oz.) crushed tomatoes

¼ teaspoon ground black pepper

1 teaspoon salt

½ teaspoon hot red pepper flakes

1 can (7 oz.) black olives, pitted

1 medium green bell pepper, seeded and cut in thin strips

1 medium red bell pepper, seeded and cut into thin strips

DIRECTIONS

In a skillet heat the oil and sauté garlic until golden, then add tomatoes, salt, black pepper and red pepper flakes. Cook for 20 minutes on medium heat, then add chopped olives and pepper strips. Cook for 10 minutes on low heat. If needed, add ½ cup water.

Cook pasta in lightly salted boiling water according to package directions, drain, and add to the sauce. And add half the grated cheese and toss gently. Transfer spaghetti to a serving bowl, garnish with cheese. Serve hot.

Makes 6 servings.

<Buon Appetito! Emilia>

GNOCCHI DI PATATE

Potato Gnocchi

INGREDIENTS

6 large potatoes

6 cups flour

4 eggs, beaten

½ teaspoon baking powder

3 cups marinara sauce

½ cup Parmesan cheese, grated

FOR GORGONZOLA SAUCE

1 pound Gorgonzola - blue cheese

DIRECTIONS

Wash and cook potatoes, unpeeled, in boiling water until soft. Peel potatoes and run through a food mill or ricer with a fine disk. In a large bowl, mix potatoes, flour and baking powder, then make a well in the center, add the eggs and work the mixture together, kneading like your would when making bread. Cover and let rest for 2 minutes.

Divide dough into 10 pieces and roll each into a half-inch rope, then cut rope into 1 inch long pieces. Sprinkle flour over the small pieces and press with a fork to give a little design.

Boil gnocchi in a large pan of salted boiling water. When gnocchi float to the top the water, they are done. Immediately remove with a slotted spoon to a colander. Serve gnocchi with marinara sauce, sprinkle Parmesan cheese and serve hot.

For a Gorgonzola sauce: In a non-stick skillet on low, warm the Gorgonzola until it is no longer lumpy and is more of a liquid. Add gnocchi to the skillet, then toss and sprinkle with Parmesan cheese. Serve hot.

<Buon Appetito!>

GNOCCHI DI CASTAGNE FROM CALABRIA

Chestnut (Flour) Gnocchi

INGREDIENTS

1 pound chestnut flour

½ pound all-purpose flour

1 teaspoon salt

1 cup warm water

4 oz. Romano cheese, grated

¼ cup olive oil

DIRECTIONS

Sift all of the flour and salt together into a good size bowl. Make a well in the center, add half of the water and start to mix with the flour. I say half the water, because is easy to add more if you need it. The gnocchi dough is suppose to be very light, so add a little flour if it becomes too thin, and then add remain water, a little at time.

Over a wooden working space, sprinkle flour and roll the dough into 1 inch thick logs. Use your thumb and roll the dough over a fork if you do not have a Calabrian crivi. Cook gnocchi in a pan of salted boiling water. Cook gnocchi for about 5 minutes, and remember to only add gnocchi when the water is boiling.

Before draining gnocchi, add 2 cups of cold water to the pot, as this will stop the cooking process faster. Transfer gnocchi to a serving platter and add oil, half of the grated cheese and gently mix. Garnish with remaining cheese and serve hot.

<From Calabria's table to yours. Enjoy! Emilia>

RICOTTA GNOCCHI

Ricotta Cheese Gnocchi

INGREDIENTS

1 pound ricotta cheese

5 cups flour

2 egg yolks

2 whole eggs

½ teaspoon baking powder

½ cup Parmesan cheese, grated

DIRECTIONS

Drain ricotta cheese into a colander or cheesecloth to drain the excess water. In a large bowl mix ricotta and flour, then add eggs and baking powder. Mix thoroughly. Cover and let rest for 5 minutes. Divide dough into 10 pieces, roll into a half-inch thick rope and cut into ½ inch pieces. Sprinkle flour over the pieces and pass a fork over the gnocchi to make a design.

Cook gnocchi in a big pot with boiling salted water. When gnocchi float to the top they are done. Immediately remove with slotted spoon to a colander. Transfer into a serving platter. Serve with your favorite sauce and sprinkle with Parmesan cheese. Serve hot.

<Buon Appetito! Emilia>

PENNE ALLA TOSCANA

Penne Tuscany Style

INGREDIENTS

1 pound penne pasta

2 tablespoons butter

2 tablespoons olive oil

1 cup onion, minced

½ teaspoon ground black pepper

1 teaspoon salt

1 egg plus 2 egg yolks

6 oz. Romano cheese, grated

2 tablespoons Italian parsley, chopped

DIRECTIONS

In a large skillet add oil and butter and sauté onion until very soft, then add salt and black pepper. Take off the heat and allow to cool.

In a small bowl, beat egg yolks and whole eggs, and then add the onions.

Cook pasta in lightly salted boiling water according to package directions, drain, and add penne to the skillet, along with the onion, egg mixture and half of the Romano cheese. Toss pasta over low heat to combine well with egg mixture.

Transfer pasta to a serving platter, sprinkle remaining cheese and garnish with chopped parsley.

Serve hot.

Makes 6 servings.

<Buon Appetito! Emilia>

SALSA AL LIMONE, AGLIO PICCANTE

Spicy Garlic & Lemon Sauce

INGREDIENTS

4 cloves of garlic, peeled and minced

3 tablespoons Italian breadcrumbs

1 tablespoon hot red chili pepper flakes

2 tablespoons Italian parsley, chopped

¼ teaspoon ground black pepper

½ teaspoon salt

3 tablespoons lemon juice

½ cup dry white wine

DIRECTIONS

In a small bowl mix all dry ingredients, then add lemon juice and wine one tablespoon at time. Stir to mix well after each tablespoon. This sauce should come out like a cream. When finished adding the recommended amount of wine, add more if mixture is too dry and add more dry ingredients if too wet.

Spread over your favorite steak or fish dishes. This can also be made days before you need it. Put sauce into plastic container and freeze until you need to use it.

<Have fun! Emilia>

SPAGHETTI ALLA CHITARRA

Egg Spaghetti

INGREDIENTS

1 pound egg spaghetti

2 frozen packages of asparagus, chopped

4 anchovies filets, packed in oil

3 cloves of garlic, peeled and chopped

3 tablespoons extra virgin olive oil

4 sage leaves

2 oz. prosciutto, cubed in small pieces

1 pound cherry tomatoes, cut in half

1 teaspoon red chili pepper flakes

¼ cup Parmesan cheese, grated

DIRECTIONS

Cook 1 package asparagus, drain and pour into an electric blender. Add anchovies, garlic, and 2 tablespoons of oil, sage leaves and 2 tablespoons of water left over from the asparagus. Blend for 2 minutes until the entire mixture becomes a creamy pesto.

In a large skillet add 1 tablespoon oil, prosciutto and the second package of asparagus. Sauté until prosciutto is light brown. Add cherry tomatoes and cook for 4 minutes; then add the mixture from the blender to the skillet and cook for 1 minute until mixture is blended together

Cook pasta in lightly salted boiling water according to package directions, drain, and add pasta to the skillet, and add chili pepper.

Toss well and transfer to a serving platter. Garnish with Parmesan cheese and serve hot.

Makes 6 servings.

<Buon Appetito! Emilia>

PENNE RIGATE CON PROSCIUTTO COTTO AL FORNO

Penne Rigate with Ham and Cheese

INGREDIENTS

1 pound penne

2 cups asparagus, chopped

2 tablespoons extra virgin olive oil

2 cloves of garlic, peeled and chopped

2 hot red chili peppers, chopped

1 teaspoon butter

¼ teaspoon ground black pepper

3 cups ham, diced

1 ½ cups fontina cheese, shredded

1 cup Swiss cheese, shredded

DIRECTIONS

Preheat oven to 350 F.

Cut asparagus into 2 inch pieces. Cook pasta in lightly salted boiling water according to package directions, and add asparagus to the pasta pot pan during the last four 4 minutes of cooking time. Drain pasta and asparagus, reserving ½ cup of the cooking water, and set aside.

Heat oil in a large skillet, add garlic and chili peppers and sauté until garlic is golden. Then add pasta with asparagus, butter, black pepper, diced ham and the cheeses to the skillet, along with ½ cup of water reserved from pasta pan. Toss gently and pour pasta mixture into a shallow 4-quart casserole dish. Cover and bake for 15 minutes. Uncover and bake for an additional 5 minutes. Serve when pasta is hot.

Makes 6 servings.

<Buon Appetito! Emilia>

TORTELLINI AL RAGU CON SALSICCIE

Tortellini Ragu

INGREDIENTS

2 packages cheese and herb tortellini

2 tablespoons olive oil

4 cloves of garlic, peeled and chopped

1 pound hot Italian turkey sausage with casing removed

1 ½ cups chicken broth

1 cup onion, sliced

3 oz. porcini mushrooms, sliced

3 oz. wild mushrooms, sliced

1 cup asparagus spears, cut 1 inch long

1 pound cherry tomatoes, halved

½ teaspoon salt

¼ teaspoon ground black pepper

¼ cup Parmesan cheese, grated

¼ cup fresh parsley, chopped

DIRECTIONS

In large skillet heat oil and sauté garlic until golden. Add turkey sausage meat and sauté until no longer pink, then add half of the chicken broth and cook for four minutes.

Cook tortellini according package directions, drain, and set aside.

While tortellini is cooking, add sliced mushrooms, tomatoes, asparagus, salt and pepper to the sausage and broth mixture. Stir for four minutes, add reaming chicken broth, and cook for 2 more minutes. Add tortellini to the skillet, toss and cook for 1 minute.

Add half the Parmesan cheese and half the chopped parsley, then toss and transfer tortellini to a serving platter. Garnish with remaining cheese and chopped parsley. Serve hot.

Makes 6 servings.

<Buon Appetito! Emilia>

PENNE ALLE AROMI DI BOSCO (FUNGHI SELVAGGI)

Penne with Wild Mushrooms

INGREDIENTS

1 pound penne pasta

2 tablespoons extra virgin olive oil

1 tablespoon unsalted butter

4 cloves of garlic, peeled and sliced

2 cups wild mushrooms, sliced

1 cup straw mushrooms, 1 (8 oz.) can (Pastine)

1 tablespoon fresh oregano, chopped

½ cup Italian parsley, chopped

6 large basil leaves, thinly sliced

1 teaspoon fresh rosemary, chopped

½ teaspoon ground black pepper

½ teaspoon salt

1 cup dry white wine

DIRECTIONS

Heat oil and butter and sauté garlic in a large skillet until golden, then add wild mushrooms and sauté on medium-low heat for 2 minutes. Add straw mushrooms, herbs, half the chopped parsley, salt and pepper. Add wine and cook on low heat for four minutes.

Cook pasta in lightly salted boiling water according to package directions, drain, transfer penne to the skillet and toss on medium heat. Put pasta in a serving bowl, garnish with chopped parsley and serve hot.

To make this a very wild dish, add 1 teaspoon hot red-chili pepper flakes.

Serve with nice cool glass of dry wine.

Makes 6 servings.

<From my kitchen to yours. Buon Appetito! Emilia>

LINGUINE ALLA GORGONZOLA

Linguine with Gorgonzola Cream

INGREDIENTS

12 oz. linguine pasta

5 oz. Gorgonzola, crumbled

½ cup light cream (panna)

1 tablespoon fresh sage, finely chopped

6 sage leaves, shredded for garnish

Pinch of salt and ground pepper

DIRECTIONS

In a large saucepan heat Gorgonzola, cream and ground black pepper until cream is hot and cheese is melted.

Cook pasta in lightly salted boiling water according to package directions, drain, transfer to the saucepan mixture, add chopped sage and toss over medium heat until linguine pasta is evenly coated. Divide linguini into separate dishes and garnish each serving with shredded sage. Serve hot.

This dish is very simple. Do not add ground cheese or other spices.

Makes 4 servings.

<Enjoy! Emilia>

FETTUCCINI CON FUNGHI PORTABELLO

Fettuccini with Portabello Mushrooms

INGREDIENTS

12 oz. fettuccini pasta

2 tablespoons extra virgin olive oil

½ cup onion, sliced

4 cloves of garlic, peeled and chopped

4 large Portabello mushrooms, washed, dried and sliced

2 tablespoons softened butter

½ teaspoon salt

½ teaspoon ground black pepper

½ cup pitted black olives, sliced

½ cup dry white wine

¼ cup Parmesan cheese, grated

½ cup Italian parsley, chopped

½ cup Parmesan cheese, shredded

DIRECTIONS

Cook pasta in lightly salted boiling water according to package directions, drain and keep warm.

While pasta is cooking, heat oil in a large skillet and sauté onion and garlic until golden. Add sliced mushrooms and sauté until tender, then add butter, salt, pepper, sliced olives and half the wine. Cook covered on low to medium heat for 2 minutes.

Add fettuccini to the skillet; add remaining wine and sprinkle with grated cheese. Toss gently and stir for 30 seconds.

Transfer fettuccini to a serving platter and garnish with shredded cheese and chopped parsley. Serve hot.

Buon Appetito! Emilia

7. MAIN COURSES

CALABRIA PARMIGIANA DI MALENZANI

Eggplant Parmigiana Calabria-style

INGREDIENTS

2 eggs, beaten

1 ½ cups breadcrumbs

2 eggplants cut crosswise into ½ inch rounds

2½ cups marinara sauce

½ cup Parmesan cheese, grated

1 cup mozzarella cheese, thinly sliced

¼ teaspoon salt

¼ teaspoon black pepper

DIRECTIONS

Preheat oven to 400 F.

Beat the eggs in a shallow dish and season with salt and pepper. In a second dish add the breadcrumbs. Dip slices of eggplant into the egg mixture then into breadcrumbs, coating each side.

Preheat the oven to 400 F. Prepare a pan with a rack set inside of it and spread eggplant slices over the rack and bake for 5 minutes on each side.

In the meantime, grease a large baking pan and spoon 1 cup of marinara sauce into the bottom, and then arrange a layer of eggplant over sauce.

Next, sprinkle with ¼ cup Parmesan cheese, ½ cup of the mozzarella slices and ½ cup marinara sauce. Repeat the layering process with the eggplant, ¼ cup of Parmesan, ½ cup of mozzarella and then ½ cup of marinara sauce. Bake uncovered for 15 to 20 minuets.

Serve with a slice of veal roast or any dish you like.

<Buon Appetito from Calabria!>

TONNO ALLA GRIGLIA

Grilled Tuna Steak

INGREDIENTS

1 lb. tuna

1 teaspoon brown sugar

1 teaspoon ginger

1 tablespoon lemon juice

1 tablespoon fat free salad dressing

1 lemon, sliced for garnish

1 teaspoon black pepper

1 tablespoon parsley, chopped

DIRECTIONS

Place tuna in a baking dish or large shallow bowl, then in a small bowl mix all of the rest of the ingredients and pour over the tuna. Turn the tuna over to coat both sides. Cover the dish and store in the refrigerator for one hour on each side, for a total of 2 hours.

Grill the fish over hot coals and baste as you cook with the leftover marinade. Garnish with lemon slices. Serve with baked potatoes or a fresh garden salad.

<Buon Appetito!>

PETTO DI POLLO CON IL BASILICO

Sliced Chicken Breast with Basil

INGREDIENTS

1 pound of chicken breasts, 4 thick slices

2 cloves of garlic, chopped

2 cups of tomatoes, peeled and cut into small cubes

1 cup fresh basil leaves, thinly sliced

1 tablespoon margarine or butter

½ cup dry white wine

DIRECTIONS

In a non-stick oven-proof pan place chicken and sauté until golden brown. Add the butter and chopped garlic and sauté until butter is melted.

While sautéing the chicken, preheat the oven to 375F.

Cover sauté pan with foil and bake for 20 minutes, then add the wine, and let cool for 20 minutes.

Put chicken and wine sauce in a serving dish and garnish with chopped basil leaves. Serve hot with plain long grain rice.

<Buon Appetito! Emilia>

TROTA AL VINO BIANCO COME LA FACEVE MAMMA

My Mother's Trout with White Wine

INGREDIENTS

4 trout fillets

¾ cup flour

1 tablespoon olive oil

2 oz. butter

½ cup yellow onion, minced

2 cloves of garlic, chopped

1 cup dry white wine

1 pound (large bunch) arugula, chopped

½ cup fresh sage, chopped

¼ teaspoon salt and black pepper to taste

DIRECTIONS

Wash the trout thoroughly and pat dry.

Add flour in a dish and coat the trout on each side. In a skillet add oil and butter and sauté onions until golden brown. Add garlic and then the trout, cooking the fillets for 5 minutes on each side. Add chopped arugola, sage, white wine, salt and pepper.

Cover and cook on medium heat for 10 minutes. Serve hot with a green salad.

Makes 4 servings.

<Buon Appetito! Emilia>

COTOLETTE DI VITELLA

Veal Cutlets

INGREDIENTS

2 eggs

¼ teaspoon black pepper

¼ teaspoon salt

¾ cup breadcrumbs

½ cup flour

1 pound veal cutlets, cut into 1 inch thick slices

2 tablespoons extra virgin olive oil

DIRECTIONS

Beat eggs with the salt and pepper. Put flour and breadcrumbs in 2 separate dishes. Pass veal into flour first, second into eggs, third into breadcrumbs.

In non-stick skillet heat oil and add veal cutlets; cook for 4 minutes on each side, not turning the cutlets more then once.

FOR CUTLETS PARMIGIANA

1 cup marinara sauce

¼ cup Parmesan cheese

½ cup grated mozzarella cheese

DIRECTIONS

In a baking pan add ½ cup the marinara sauce, add veal cutlets over the sauce, and sprinkle some Parmesan cheese. Add another ½ cup marinara sauce over the veal and top with mozzarella cheese.

Pre-heat the oven to 375 F. Bake for 6 minutes, or until the mozzarella starts to melt and become golden. This dish can also be made with chicken or turkey.

Makes 6 servings.

<Buon Appetito! Emilia>

POLLO PICCATA ALL`AROME DI LIMONE

Lemon Chicken Piccata

INGREDIENTS

6 boneless, skinless chicken breast halves

¼ teaspoon salt

¼ teaspoon black pepper

2 tablespoons extra virgin olive oil

4 cloves of garlic, peeled and chopped

3 lemons, peeled and sliced

2 tablespoons parsley, chopped

1-¾ cups dry white wine

DIRECTIONS

Rinse chicken breasts and dry with paper towel. Season chicken breast with salt and pepper. In non-stick skillet heat oil and sauté garlic until golden brown, then add chicken and cook for 4 minutes, turning once. Transfer chicken to a warm platter.

Add lemon slices and 1 teaspoon parsley, chopped to the skillet and cook for 1 minute. Then increase heat, stir in wine and simmer for 5 minutes or until liquid is reduced by about half.

Return chicken to the pan and cook for 2 minutes, turning once to heat the chicken through. Transfer chicken to a serving platter and sprinkle with the remaining parsley. Serve with a green salad or rice.

Makes 6 servings.

<Have fun! Emilia>

POLLO ALLA GRIGLIA CON VEGETALE ARROSTITE

Grilled Vegetable Salad with Roasted Chicken

INGREDIENTS

1 green pepper, seeded and cut into small strips

1 yellow pepper, seeded and cut into small strips

1 red pepper, seeded and cut into small strips

1 medium zucchini, cut into thick slices

6 cups assorted salad greens, cut into bits and kept chilled

1 cup provolone cheese, cut into cubes

6 oz. roast chicken, cut into small cubes

FOR THE VINAIGRETTE

2 tablespoons lemon juice

1 tablespoon lemon peel

2 tablespoons balsamic vinegar

¼ teaspoon oregano flakes

2 tablespoons Parmesan cheese, grated

DIRECTIONS

In a large bowl toss all of the vegetable with the vinaigrette. Remove with slotted spoon, reserving the dressing for use later. Grill 15 minutes or until tender, turning the vegetables frequently. Return vegetables to the reserved dressing. This can be made 2 to 3 days in advance. Cover and refrigerate for 2 days.

Divide salad greens among six plates and use a slotted spoon to distribute the grilled vegetables evenly. Add cubed chicken and provolone. Garnish with Parmesan cheese, and serve vinaigrette on the side if desired.

Makes 6 servings.

<Enjoy! Emilia>

SALCICCIE PICCANTE CON RISO GIALLO

Hot Sausage with Yellow Rice Dinner

INGREDIENTS

2 tablespoons vegetable oil

1 cup piccante (hot) Italian tomato or pasta sauce

3 Italian piccante (hot) sausages, sliced into rings

½ cup onion, minced

4 cups yellow rice, rinsed

1-¾ cups cold water

¼ teaspoon salt

¼ teaspoon black pepper

DIRECTIONS

Heat the vegetable oil in a 5-quart pot over high heat, then the onion and sauté until golden. Add sausage rings; reduce heat to medium and cook for 3 minutes. Add sauce, rice water and salt, stirring for 1 minute. Cover pot and continue cooking over medium heat for 5 minutes, stirring occasionally.

Lower heat and simmer for 20 minutes, stirring 2 or 3 times to prevent rice from sticking to the pot. Serve with red kidney beans and a green salad.

For a quick and easy version, simply prepare an 8 oz. package of Spanish style yellow rice on stovetop, according to package directions. When rice is half cooked add sliced sausage with sauce, and finish cooking.

Makes 6 servings.

<Buon Appetito! Emilia>

PETTO DI POLLO CON FORMAGIO FONTINA

Chicken Breast with Fontina Cheese

INGREDIENTS

4 chicken breasts

¼ teaspoon salt

¼ teaspoon black pepper

4 tablespoons butter

6 oz. dry white wine

2 tablespoons Chianti wine

8 slices smoked Fontina cheese

DIRECTIONS

Dredge chicken breasts in flour seasoned with salt and pepper. Melt butter in a sauté pan and cook chicken breasts on each side approximately 5 minutes until cooked through and golden brown on outside. While you are doing this, preheat the broiler.

Remove the chicken breasts from the sauté pan and arrange them in an ovenproof baking dish. Add white wine and Chianti wine to pan juices and simmer over low heat for about 6 minutes.

Pour pan juices over the chicken breasts and layer fontina cheese slices on top of the chicken. Broil for 2 minutes until cheese is bubbly.

Makes 4 servings.

<Enjoy! Emilia>

POLLO E RISO

Chicken & Rice

INGREDIENTS

10 oz. long grain rice

2 cups arugula leaves, chopped

6 half chicken breasts, marinated in your choice of dressing

2 tablespoons extra virgin olive oil

1 cup Italian plum tomatoes, seeded and chopped

1 cup red onion, sliced

4 cloves of garlic, peeled and minced

½ teaspoon salt

½ teaspoon ground black pepper

½ cup mozzarella cheese slice and shredded

DIRECTIONS

Cook rice according to package directions. Four minutes before the end of the cooking time add the chopped arugula and let simmer for the time remaining. Preheat your broiler at this time.

In a large skillet (with a handle that can withstand the broiler) sauté chicken breasts until each side is no longer pink. Transfer chicken breasts to a dish and add the onion, garlic, salt, pepper and chopped tomatoes to the skillet. Cook over medium heat for 5 minutes.

Place the chicken breasts over the tomato sauce. Cover with mozzarella cheese and transfer skillet from top of the stove to under the broiler until the mozzarella is melted at least 2 minutes. Serve over the rice.

Makes 6 servings.

<Buon Appetito!>

ARROSTO CON ZUCCHINI

Prime Rib & Zucchini

INGREDIENTS

3 Italian zucchini, sliced

2 tablespoons oil

2 clove garlic peel and chopped

¾ cup onion, minced

1 cup celery, chopped into ½ inch pieces

1 teaspoon ground black pepper

3 slice Italian bread cut in 1 inch cube and toasted

1 tablespoon Mrs. Dash seasoning

1 chili red pepper, chopped

½ cup dry red wine

6 prime rib steaks

½ cup fresh parsley, chopped

DIRECTIONS

Cut zucchini lengthwise, take the seeds out with a melon scoop, and cut into 1-½ strips.

In a large skillet add oil and sauté garlic until golden, then add onions, zucchini, celery, toasted bread, wine, black pepper and all of the spices except the parsley which is saved for garnish at the end and the wine. Cook until vegetables are tender, about 4 to 5 minutes.

Spice the meat with salt and black pepper. Grill the steaks for 5 minutes on each side. Serve with zucchini sauce with a baked potato and green salad. If you like little more spice, add ½ teaspoon red chili pepper flakes to the zucchini mixture while cooking.

Makes 6 servings.

<Have fun! Emilia>

FILETTO DI MAIALE ALLA GRIGLIA

Grilled Pork Chops

INGREDIENTS

6 pork chops

2 tablespoons vegetable oil

¼ teaspoon salt

½ teaspoon black pepper

2 tablespoons red wine vinegar

6 cloves of garlic, peeled and chopped

¾ cup soy sauce

1 teaspoon ground ginger

DIRECTIONS

In a large bowl, combine all the ingredients, mix with fork and add the pork chops, cover with foil pepper and refrigerate for 4 hours or overnight.

Drain and discard the marinade: grill pork chops on medium heat for 5 minute each side. Serve with long grain wild rice or roasted potatoes.

Makes 6 servings.

<Buon Appetito!>

SALCICCIE CON FUNGUI PORCINI

Sausage & Porcini Mushrooms

INGREDIENTS

6 links Italian hot sausage

2 teaspoons olive oil

4 cloves of garlic, peeled and chopped

½ cup onion, minced

1 28 oz. can peeled and chopped tomatoes

¼ cup parsley, chopped

½ cup basil leaves, chopped

½ teaspoon oregano flakes

½ cup white wine

2 cans porcini mushrooms (Pastine)

DIRECTIONS

Cut sausage into ½ inch rings. Sauté sausage in a large skillet until brown. Drain the fat from the pan; add 2 tablespoons of oil, the garlic and onions. Sauté while stirring for 4 minutes. Add chopped tomatoes, parsley, basil, oregano and wine and cook for 7 more minutes.

Add mushrooms to the skillet. Simmer for 5 minutes. Serve as an appetizer or on top of your favorite pizza.

<As a lower calorie and fat alternative use turkey or chicken. Enjoy! Emilia>

COSCETTE D'AGNELLO ALLA ROSAMARINA

Rosemary Lamb Shanks

INGREDIENTS

6 lamb shanks

6 cloves of garlic, peeled and chopped

3 tablespoons rosemary chopped

3 tablespoons mixed herbs – use your favorites

½ teaspoon salt

1 teaspoon ground black pepper

2 tablespoon oil

1 tablespoon garlic powder 1 cup dry white wine

DIRECTIONS

With sharp knife make small incisions in the lamb shanks and insert 1 clove of chopped garlic into each. In a small bowl mix salt, pepper, rosemary, black pepper, garlic powder, and herb mix. Rub on the lamb shanks so that all surfaces are covered.

Cover the lamb with foil and marinate for 2 hours in the refrigerator.

Preheat oven to 375 F. and place the lamb in a roasting pan, oil, wine, and bake for 30 minutes. Then cover foil and bake for 20 more minutes.

Serve with asparagus, baked potatoes and a green salad.

Makes 6 servings.

<Buon Appetito! Emilia>

PESCE AL MAICROONDA

Microwave Salmon & Scallops Dinner

INGREDIENTS

2 pounds fresh salmon

1 cup dry white wine

1 ½ cups fish stock

1 ½ lemon, thinly sliced

1 tablespoon lemon juice

¼ teaspoon ground black pepper

2 tablespoons butter

2 cloves of garlic, peeled and minced

1 pound bay scallops

½ teaspoon salt

¼ teaspoon black pepper

½ cup fresh torn Italian parsley

DIRECTIONS

Place salmon in a large microwave dish; add lemon, wine, fish stock and black pepper. Cover salmon with plastic wrap and puncture to vent. Cook on high power for 20 minutes.

In a small skillet add butter and garlic and sauté until golden. Add scallops and stir for 2 minutes. Transfer salmon to a serving dish and add scallops over the salmon. Garnish with chopped parsley.

Serve with cooked asparagus or a mixed green salad.

Makes 6 servings.

<Enjoy! Emilia>

ARROSTO AL FORNO

Roasted Prime Rib

INGREDIENTS

5 pound prime rib roast

½ teaspoon rosemary flakes

½ teaspoon ground black pepper

½ teaspoon salt

1 cup dry white wine

1 tablespoon all purpose flour

DIRECTIONS

Preheat oven to 400 F.

In a small bowl mix wine, salt, pepper and rosemary Place the prime rib into a roasting pan and pour the wine mixture over the roast. Baste every ten minutes for 30 minutes, then reduce heat to 350 F. Cook the roast for 20 minutes per pound, or until the meat thermometer reaches 160 degrees for medium or 170 degrees for well done when inserted into the center of the roast.

Remove roast from the pan, cover with foil and let stand 5 minutes before slicing. This will make this roast, or any other roast for that matter, more moist and juicy when served.

While letting the roast rest, add flour to the roasting pan, stirring constantly until the gravy is thickened. Serve with roasted potatoes and carrots.

<Buon Appetito! Emilia>

FILETTO DI MAIALE CON FUNGHI A CIPOLLA

Pork Tenderloin with Mushrooms and Onion

INGREDIENTS

2 tablespoons olive oil

3 cloves of garlic, peeled and chopped

½ cup yellow onions, chopped

1 ½ pounds of pork tenderloin, cut into 1 ½ inch cubes

3 cups red, green, and yellow peppers cut into 1½ strips

2 cans 14 oz each, porcini mushrooms

¼ teaspoon ground black pepper

½ teaspoon salt

¼ teaspoon rosemary flakes

2 bay leaves

1 tablespoon balsamic vinegar

2 tablespoons all-purpose flour

DIRECTIONS

Heat oil in a large skillet, add chopped garlic and sauté until golden. Then add onions and cook until tender. Add pork tenderloin, stir until browned, and then add all remaining ingredients except the balsamic vinegar and flour. Cook at a low simmer until peppers are tender.

Stir in balsamic vinegar and flour for about 1 minute until you have a thick sauce on the bottom of the skillet. Serve with long grain rice or risotto.

Makes 6 servings.

<Enjoy! Emilia>

FILETTO DI MAIALE IMBOTTITO DA EMILIA

Emilia's Stuffed Pork Tenderloin

INGREDIENTS

Stuffing:

1 cup Italian breadcrumbs

1 egg, beaten

¼ cup Italian parsley, chopped

½ teaspoon salt

½ teaspoon ground black pepper

2 tablespoons of Romano cheese, grated

1 tablespoon olive oil

4 cloves of garlic, peeled and chopped

2 large portabella mushrooms, stems removed and thinly chopped

Meat and Sauce:

2 pound pork tenderloin

2 bay leaves

1 ¼ cup white wine

2 tablespoons cornstarch

DIRECTIONS

Preheat oven to 400 F.

In a large bowl mix all of the stuffing ingredients thoroughly.

With a sharp knife butterfly the pork tenderloin. Put the stuffing mixture on the meat, leaving a 1 inch border without the mixture.

Roll the tenderloin like you roll a braciola, then secure with string. Sauté the tenderloin in a skillet until golden and brown.

Transfer the tenderloin to a roasting pan, and then add wine, bay leaves and cover with foil. Place in preheated oven for 25 minutes. Uncover roasting pan, turn the roast over and bake for another 20 minutes. Insert meat thermometer into thickest part of tenderloin to make sure that it registers 170 F.

Let stand 5 minutes before cutting, then cut strings and slice the roast into ½ inch thick pieces. Add cornstarch to the wine sauce in the roasting pan, stirring constantly until the sauce has thickened.

Serve tenderloin on a serving plate with baked potatoes and steamed mixed vegetables.

Makes 6 servings.

<If you cook with fun, you will enjoy your meals! Emilia>

COSCIA D'ANGELLO CON ROSAMARINO E AGLIO

Garlic & Rosemary Leg of Lamb

INGREDIENTS

1 leg of lamb, about 6 pounds

8 cloves of garlic, peeled and sliced in half

1 cup fresh rosemary, coarsely chopped

2 tablespoons Italian herbs

1 teaspoon salt

1 teaspoon black pepper

¾ cup diced ham or Prosciutto

2 cup red wine

2 tablespoons cornstarch

DIRECTIONS

Preheat oven to 400 F.

Use a sharp knife to make 16 slits in the leg of lamb and insert 1 piece of garlic and a pinch of rosemary in each slit. Mix all the herbs, salt and black pepper and rub all over the leg lamb.

Heat a large skillet and sauté the ham or Prosciutto, then add the leg of lamb and sauté until brown. Transfer lamb to a large roasting pan, add 1 cup of the wine, and bake for 20 minutes, then turn the roast over, cover and bake for another 20 minutes, or until the thermometer registers 160 F. Let the roast sit for 5 minutes, then slice lamb ½ inch tick.

Transfer roasting pan onto the stove over medium heat. Add remaining 1 cup of wine and cornstarch, stirring constantly until the sauce thickens to gravy. Transfer sliced lamb onto a serving platter and pour gravy over the lamb. Serve with cooked asparagus, small sautéed red potatoes and a green salad.

Makes 8 servings.

<Enjoy and have fun! Emilia>

EMILIA VITELLA SCALOPPINE RIPIENI

Emilia's Stuffed Veal Scaloppini

INGREDIENTS

8 slices of veal, ½ inch thick

3 tablespoons olive oil for sautés the veal

½ cup olive oil for the sauce

2/ tablespoons mince garlic

¼ cup mince onion,

4 tablespoon pitted green olives thinly sliced

4 tablespoons cappers in vinegar

2 anchovies, thinly sliced

2 eggs beaten

2 tablespoon Parmesan cheese, grated

¼ teaspoon ground black pepper

½ teaspoon salt

1 15 oz. can crushed tomatoes

¼ teaspoon oregano flakes

2 fresh basil leaves, chopped

DIRECTIONS

First butterfly the veal chops, then sprinkle with black pepper and salt. In a small bowl, add breadcrumbs, Parmesan cheese, parsley, half the garlic, chopped olives, and 1 teaspoon oil. Divide mixture in equal portion over the veal. Roll veal, using toothpicks to secure the ends.

In a dish add flour and dredge each slice of veal into flour, then into eggs beat, and then into breadcrumbs. In no stick skillet heat oil and add scaloppini. Sauté over medium heat until golden and brown.

Add garlic and onion and sauté until golden, then add crushed tomatoes, chopped basil leaves, and a pinch salt and black pepper. Cook for 20 minutes at a low simmer until veal is tender. Serve with green beans and potato salad.

Makes 4 servings.

<Buon Appetito! Emilia>

SALSICCIE E VEGETALE

Sausage & Mixed Vegetables

INGREDIENTS

½ cup olive oil

1 pound Italian hot sausage, cut into ½ inch rings

6 medium red potatoes, cut into 1-½ inch cubes

1 large green bell pepper, seeded and cut into 2 inch strips

1 cup porcini mushrooms

1 teaspoon salt

½ teaspoon ground black pepper

2 cloves of garlic, peeled and chopped

1 medium yellow onion, sliced into 1-inch strips

2 tablespoon parsley, chopped

½ cup tomatoes, peeled and chopped

DIRECTIONS

Preheat oven to 400 F.

In a large non-stick ovenproof pan, add ½ of the oil, potatoes, sausage, peppers, onion, garlic, mushrooms and salt and black pepper. Mix well and add chopped tomatoes, parsley and remaining oil.

Bake for 30 minutes, stir with a wooden spatula, cover with foil, and bake for another 10 minutes.

Serve hot for lunch or as a side dish with dinner.

Makes 6 servings.

My mother, Russo Maria Concetta, made this dish for our family, and we loved it. (Although I do like to add some of my own ingredients from time to time.)

<From my Mother to me and now to you. Enjoy! Emilia>

FILETTO DI VITELLA ALLA GRIGLIA

Grilled or Broiled Peppercorn T-bone Steak

INGREDIENTS

4 T- bone veal steaks, about 1 pound each

4 cloves of garlic, peeled and chopped

2 tablespoons black peppercorns, crushed

½ teaspoon lemon juice

1 tablespoon Worcestershire sauce

1 tablespoon salt

DIRECTIONS

Rub garlic, black pepper, Worcestershire and lemon juice onto each side of the veal steaks and let marinate in the refrigerator for 2 hours.

Grill veal 5 to 6 inches from the heat. For medium, cook 10 minutes total, turning once about 5 minutes each side.

When done sprinkle with salt and black pepper. Serve with rice or a green salad.

Makes 4 servings.

<Have fun! Emilia>

AGNELLO ALLA CONTADINA

Country Lamb

INGREDIENTS

3 pounds of lamb, cut into pieces

2 pounds small red potatoes

2 cloves of garlic, peeled and chopped

1 yellow onion, quartered

1 teaspoon rosemary flakes

½ cup olive oil

½ teaspoon salt

½ teaspoon ground black pepper

2 tablespoons red wine

DIRECTIONS

Preheat oven to 375 F.

Place lamb and potatoes in a large oven-proof skillet. Sprinkle spices and pour oil and wine into the pan. Mix to coat lamb and potatoes evenly.

Cover with a sheet of foil and bake for 1 hour, then uncover and bake for 10 more minutes, until potatoes and lamb are golden and brown.

Serve hot.

Makes 6 servings.

<Buon Appetito! Emilia>

TORTA DI ZUCCHINI

Zucchini Quiche

INGREDIENTS

3 cups finely shredded zucchini

4 eggs, beaten

1 cup biscuit mix

½ cup Parmesan cheese, grated

3 oz Swiss cheese, shredded

½ cup extra virgin olive oil

1 cup green onions, cut into ½ inch pieces

2 tablespoons fresh parsley, chopped

DIRECTIONS

Preheat oven to 350 F.

Combine all the ingredients in a large bowl and pour into a greased 9-inch quiche dish. Bake uncovered for 35 to 45 minutes. Insert a knife at the center of the quiche; if the knife comes out clean, then the quiche is done.

Let stand 5 to 10 minutes before serving.

<Enjoy! Emilia>

ARROSTO DI VITELLO OR AGNELLO

Basic Veal or Lamb Roast

INGREDIENTS

2 tablespoons rosemary, chopped

1 tablespoon ground black pepper

2 tablespoons thyme, chopped

4 cloves of garlic, chopped

½ cup olive oil

1 teaspoon salt

1 veal roast, which is about 8 veal, chops

4 cups potatoes, peeled and quartered

2 cups baby carrots

DIRECTIONS

Preheat oven to 375 F.

In a small bowl, add the first 6 ingredients and mix well. With your hand rub this pesto all around the roast.

Place roast fat side up in the oven for 40 minutes. Add the vegetables and let roast for an additional 30 minutes.

Before you take the roast from the oven double-check the temperature with a thermometer. 160-165 F. for rare/medium and 165-170 for medium/well done. Remove roast from the oven, cover with foil and let stand 10 minutes before serving.

This roast is nice when served over long grain wild rice.

Makes 8 servings.

<Buon Appetito! Emilia>

ERBE MISTE PER CARNI

Herb Blend for Poultry

INGREDIENTS

2 tablespoons parley flakes

1 tablespoon lemon zest

2 tablespoons thyme

2 tablespoons chopped rosemary or dry flakes

1 tablespoon garlic powder

1 tablespoon salt

1 tablespoon ground black pepper

DIRECTIONS

In a small bowl, mix all the ingredients. Sprinkle over poultry during cooking or use in a shaker at the table.

Store any extra spice in a tightly covered glass container in the refrigerator.

You can make this a day ahead to save time.

<Enjoy! Emilia>

FRITTATA CON BROCCOLETTE DI RAPI

Broccoli Rapi Frittata

INGREDIENTS

2 tablespoons extra virgin olive oil

1 tablespoon onion, minced

6 eggs

¾ cup fontina cheese, shredded

½ teaspoon salt

½ teaspoon black pepper

¾ cup cooked ham, diced

2 cups fresh broccoli rapi, chopped

DIRECTIONS

In a non-stick frying pan, heat oil and sauté onion until golden brown. In a bowl, beat the eggs and cheese together with the salt and pepper. Add cooked ham and pour over the onion mix, cook on low for 2 minutes, and then add rapi to the pan and mix all tougher.

Add the egg mixture and cook until the bottom of the frittata is firm and golden. Place a flat round dish on top of the pan, turn the frittata over onto the dish, and then place the frittata back into the frying pan. Cook for 4 more minutes on low heat, or until frittata is cooked through.

If you cannot turn frittata with a dish, then be sure to start with an oven-proof skillet. Preheat oven to 375 F. and bake for 5 to 8 minutes, or until frittata is solid on the top. Place on a serving dish and let stand for 5 minutes before cutting.

Serve hot or cool.

Makes 6 servings.

<Cook for the family and yourself. Emilia>

FRITTATA CON ASPARACI

Asparagus Omelet

INGREDIENTS

6 eggs

1 pound asparagus

1 oz. butter

2 tablespoons olive oil

½ teaspoon salt

½ cup Parmesan cheese, grated

DIRECTIONS

Clean asparagus and cut into 1 inch long pieces. Use only the green parts, not the tougher stem ends.

Beat eggs, salt and cheese together in a bowl and add asparagus pieces. In a large non-stick skillet heat the butter and oil and pour the mixture into the pan.

Cook over medium low heat, using a fork periodically to make the mixture goes to bottom.

When the bottom is golden, put flat dish over the skillet, turn frittata over and gently put back into the skillet. Let cook until all the moisture from the eggs is gone.

If you cannot flip the frittata, then use an oven-proof skillet to start with and preheat the oven to 375 F. After the first side is done, instead of flipping upside down, bake frittata uncovered until the top is golden and dry.

Place on a serving dish and let stand for 5 minutes before cutting.

Makes 4 servings.

<Buon Appetito! Emilia>

Emilia Fusco

FRITTATA DI PASTA E SALSICCIE PICCANTE

Pasta and Hot Sausage Frittata

INGREDIENTS

4 hot Italian sausage links

12 eggs

1 cup roasted red bell pepper, thinly sliced

½ cup olive oil

½ pound spaghetti

2 tablespoons butter

¾ cup Parmesan cheese, grated

½ teaspoon ground black pepper

½ cup fresh basil leaves, chopped

DIRECTIONS

Remove sausage from the casings and sauté in a skillet over medium heat until golden and brown. Cook spaghetti pasta according to package directions. When spaghetti is done, drain and toss with butter, Parmesan cheese, and ground black pepper and set aside to cool.

Break eggs into a large mixing bowl and beat the eggs for 1 minute with a hand mixer. Add pasta and toss well to combine eggs and pasta evenly.

Heat some oil in a large non-stick skillet and add half the pasta mixture.

Spread roasted peppers and cooked sausage evenly across the frittata, and then add the remaining pasta mix. Cook on medium heat until the bottom of frittata is golden and light brown.

Using a large flat round dish, place it over the skillet and flip frittata up side down.

Return to the skillet and allow the other side to cook until golden and light brown.

If you cannot flip the frittata, then use an oven-proof skillet and preheat the oven to 375 F.

After the first side is done, instead to flipping upside down, bake frittata uncovered until the top is golden light brown.

Transfer frittata onto a serving dish, and after letting rest for 5 minutes, cut like you would a pizza or a cake. Garnish with chopped basil leaves.

Serve at brunch or cut into small pieces for a cocktail party.

This dish is Calabrese style, and we make it on the Monday after Easter.

Makes 12 servings.

<Enjoy! Emilia>

COPPA DI RISO AL TONNO E VEGETALI

Rice Dish With Tuna & Vegetables

INGREDIENTS

2 pounds Arborio rice

6 tablespoons vinegar

2 tablespoons mayonnaise

3 tablespoons extra virgin olive oil

8 oz. tuna packed in oil

1 cup peppers in vinegar, chopped

½ cup carrots, shredded

½ cup cappers packed in oil

½ cup pitted black olives

½ cup pitted green olives

10 filet anchovy 10 filet anchovy fillets

4 large tomatoes, quartered

DIRECTIONS

Cook rice according to package directions. When rice is cooked, drain and rinse under cool water. Let cool well before you mix with ingredients.

In small bowl mix vinegar, oil and mayonnaise. In a large bowl add the rice, tuna, carrots, olives, peppers and capers and toss well. If you have a small party, divide rice into 2 bowls. Add 5 sliced anchovies on top the rice in each bowl, and around the edges use half of the tomatoes in each bowl. Decorate top with chopped parsley.

Makes 12 servings.

<Enjoy! Emilia>

CONIGLIO ALLA PANCETTA

Rabbit with Bacon

INGREDIENTS

1 rabbit, chopped in pieces

3 oz. bacon or pancetta, cut in small cubes

2 tablespoons olive oil

3 clove garlic peel and chopped

4 bay leaves

½ teaspoon salt

¼ teaspoon fresh ground black pepper

½ teaspoon rosemary, chopped

2 tablespoons parsley, chopped

½ cup dry white wine

DIRECTIONS

Use fresh herbs if you can. Wash rabbit and dry with paper towel. In a large skillet add rabbit pieces and sauté on medium heat until golden brown about 20 minutes. Add oil and garlic to the skillet and sauté until garlic is golden, and then add all remaining ingredients. Cook on low heat, partially covered, for 35 minutes.

Check rabbit every now and again. If looks too dry add 3 more tablespoons of white wine at a time and continue to let simmer at low heat. Serve with potatoes, baked or fried and a green salad.

Makes 4 servings.

<Buon Appetito! Emilia>

CONIGLIO RIPIENO SENSA OSSA

Stuffed Boneless Rabbit

INGREDIENTS

1 young rabbit

1 cup breadcrumbs

½ cup parsley, chopped

1 teaspoon ground black pepper

½ teaspoon salt

1 teaspoon fresh rosemary, chopped

1 egg

2 tablespoons olive oil

3 cloves of garlic, finely chopped

DIRECTIONS

Remove the bones from the rabbit then boil them in a pan with 3 quarts of water and save the broth. (If you can't de-bone the rabbit, then ask your butcher to take the bones out for you.)

In a small bowl mix all ingredients except the garlic. Put half of the mixture in the center of the rabbit and use string to keep the cavity closed. Rub the remaining half of the herb mix on the outside of the rabbit.

Heat oil in a non-stick skillet and sauté garlic and rabbit on both sides until golden brown. Add 1 cup of the reserved broth, cover and cook for 20 minutes on low heat. Cut rabbit into ¾ inch slices and spoon remaining juices from the skillet over the dish. Serve over rice or Italian potato salad.

Makes 6 servings.

<Buon Appetito! Emilia>

INVOLTINI DI VITELLO

Veal Rolls

INGREDIENTS

6 large veal scaloppini, about 3 oz. each

2 tablespoons olive oil

2 tablespoons butter

3 clove garlic peel and chopped

6 oz. lean ground beef

2 oz. ham cut into very small pieces

2 tablespoons Parmesan cheese, grated

2 eggs

½ teaspoon fresh rosemary, finely chopped

1 teaspoon fresh sage, chopped

½ teaspoon salt

½ teaspoon ground black pepper

½ cup dry white wine

DIRECTIONS

Heat 1 tablespoon of oil and 1 tablespoon of butter in a non-stick skillet. Sauté ground beef and garlic until beef is not longer pink. Add ham and sauté for 1 minute.

Remove beef from the stove and transfer to a medium-sized bowl. Add cheese, eggs, rosemary, salt, pepper and chopped sage and mix well. Divide mixture into 6 portions and spoon over the veal. Roll up the veal cutlets and secure with toothpicks.

Heat remaining butter and oil in the same non-stick skillet and sauté veal until golden and brown on each side. Add wine and a pinch of rosemary leaves. Cover and cook on medium heat for 30 minutes. Serve dish over rice or Italian potato salad.

Makes 5 servings.

<Enjoy! Emilia>

AGNELLO ALLA CATANZARESE

Lamb Catanzaro Style (SOUTHERN ITALY)

INGREDIENTS

1 leg of lamb

1 cup flour

1 teaspoon salt

1 teaspoon ground black pepper

¼ cup olive oil

4 cloves of garlic, peeled and chopped

1 tablespoon fresh rosemary, chopped

½ cup red wine

2 red chili peppers, seed and chopped (optional)

2 tablespoons anchovy filets packed in oil, chopped (optional)

3 oz. capers, packed in oil

2 tablespoons parsley, chopped

DIRECTIONS

Cut lamb into small pieces and season with salt and pepper. In a large plastic bag add flour and cut lamb. Shake well until lamb is well coat with flour.

In large skillet heat oil and sauté garlic until golden brown. Add lamb and rosemary. Cook on medium heat for 5 minutes, then add wine and cook at low simmer for 20 minutes.

Transfer the meat to serving platter and sprinkle with the chopped anchovies, capers and parsley. Add the juice form the skillet. Serve hot as first dish with a green salad or with any side dish you prefer.

Makes 8 servings.

<Buon Appetito! Emilia>

BACCALA' A LESSO

Boiled Cod

INGREDIENTS

3 pounds cod fillets, cut into cubes

½ lemon, sliced

¼ cup olive oil

½ teaspoon ground black pepper

¼ cup fresh parsley, chopped

2 cloves of garlic, peeled and chopped

DIRECTIONS

Wash and dry fillets or scale and cut fish into pieces. Bring a large pan of water to a boil, add fish and reduce heat to low. Cook for 5 minutes. Drain using a colander, and transfer fish onto a large flat serving dish.

Top fish with chopped parsley, chopped garlic and oil and serve with lemon wedges or slices. If you like, cook some asparagus and potato salad for side dishes.

<This dish is always on our table at Christmas Eve. Emilia>

GAMBERI IN AGRODOLCE

Sweet & Sour Shrimp

INGREDIENTS

30 jumbo shrimp, cleaned

1 lemon cut into slices

½ teaspoon salt

1 tablespoon butter

2 cloves of garlic, peeled and chopped

2 anchovies packed in oil, chopped

3 tablespoons white vinegar

½ cup capers packed in oil

1 ½ tablespoons sugar

DIRECTIONS

In a large pan with boiling water add lemon, shrimp and salt. Boil for 5 minutes or until shrimp are pink.

In a skillet heat butter and garlic. Sauté until golden, then add anchovies and capers and sauté for 30 seconds longer. Add vinegar and sugar, and then stir to dissolve sugar and take the skillet off of the stove.

Drain shrimp, transfer to a serving platter, and pour the anchovy sauce over the meal. Serve as a cocktail, a snack or a second dish with rice.

<Enjoy! Emilia>

ZEPPOLE DI BACCALA'

Fried Codfish

INGREDIENTS

1 cup warm water

3 cups flour

1 egg, beaten

½ teaspoon salt

1 teaspoon dried yeast

1 pound cod fish

DIRECTIONS

In a large bowl add flour, make well in the center, then and add salt and egg. Mix yeast into ½ cup warm water and add to the well in the flour. Mix thoroughly, like you would make soft bread dough, but this dough is even more softened. It's more like a batter. Cover and let rise for 1 hour.

In a pan with 4 cups boiling water cook fish for 2 minutes. Remove fish with a slotted spoon and shred in small pieces with your hands. Add fish into the dough and mix.

In a frying pan add oil, and when the oil is hot use a dinner spoon to spoon the dough into the oil. Fry zeppoli until golden each side. Transfer zeppoli to a plate covered with paper towels to dry the excess oil. Eat warm or cool.

This is a hometown tradition to make for Christmas Eve and New Years.

<Buon Appetito! Emilia>

TROTA AI FUNGHI

Trout with Mushrooms

INGREDIENTS

4 large trout, about 1 pound each

½ cup flour

3 oz. butter

3 cloves of garlic, peeled and chopped

2 tablespoon olive oil

4 large Portobello mushrooms, sliced

½ teaspoon salt

½ teaspoon ground black pepper

½ cup fresh Italian parsley, chopped

2 tablespoons breadcrumbs

DIRECTIONS

Preheat oven to 375 F.

Cut off trout head, slice the soft under-side and take out the insides and clean well. (Or purchase fresh fillets at the grocery store.) Wash and dry trout thoroughly after cleaning. Put the flour in a dish and coat trout on each side. In skillet heat ½ the butter, oil and sauté ½ the garlic until golden.

Add trout and cook on low heat for 5 minutes on each side until golden brown.

Meanwhile, in a large ovenproof skillet melt the remaining butter and sauté the rest of the garlic until golden.

Add the mushrooms, salt, black pepper and parsley, and cook for 10 minutes. Add the trout over the mushrooms and cover with the breadcrumbs. Spray the top quickly with a vegetable oil and bake until golden and brown, about 2 minutes or until breadcrumbs are golden and light brown.

Serve over a dish of long grain rice.

Makes 4 servings.

<Buon Appetito! Emilia>

TROTA AL VINO ROSSO

Trout in Red Wine

INGREDIENTS

4 trout, about 1 pound each

1 medium onion, minced

¾ cup chopped celery

2 tablespoons butter

2 tablespoons olive oil

2 bay leaves

¼ cup fresh parsley, chopped

½ teaspoon salt

½ teaspoon ground black pepper

1 cups red table wine

½ cup fish stock

DIRECTIONS

Preheat oven to 375 F.

Cut trout head, slice the soft under-side and take out the insides and clean well. (Or purchase fresh fillets at the grocery store.) Wash and dry trout thoroughly after cleaning.

In a skillet, heath butter and oil, add onion, and sauté for I minute, add celery, half the parsley, salt and pepper, add fish stock and cook until the stock is almost dry. Grease a bake dish, add trout, and cover with vegetables mixture.

Add wine, bay leaves and bake uncover for 15 to 20 minutes, or until vegetables are tender.

Serve hot next to a dish wild rice and green beans.

<Buon Appetito! Emilia>

POMODORI RIPIENI AL PESCE

Seafood Stuffed Tomato

INGREDIENTS

6 large ripe tomatoes

1 large carrot, thinly sliced

8 oz. bay scallops

½ cup onion, minced

2 oz. pitted green olives chopped

2 tablespoons basil leaves, chopped

2 tablespoons Romano cheese, grated

2 tablespoons Parmesan cheese, grated

½ teaspoon salt

¼ teaspoon ground black pepper

2 tablespoons breadcrumbs

2 tablespoons fresh parsley, chopped

2 tablespoons olive oil

½ cup boiling water

DIRECTIONS

Preheat oven at 375 F.

Wash and dry tomatoes. Cut off the tops, spoon out all the seeds and soft parts inside and save the shells. In a pan with boiling water and pinch salt add carrots, and boil until very tender. While the carrots are boiling, wash and dry the bay scallops and put in a large bowl.

Add cooked carrots, chopped olives, minced onion, chopped basil leaves, 1 tablespoon Romano cheese, 1 tablespoon the Parmesan cheese, salt and pepper. Mix well and spoon mixture into tomatoes. Mix breadcrumbs, parsley and remaining cheese and sprinkle over the stuffed tomatoes.

In a baking dish add ½ cup of boiling water, 2 tablespoons of oil and bake tomatoes for 10 to 15 minutes. Serve hot, next to a green salad.

Makes 6 servings.

<This is fun! Enjoy! Emilia>

Emilia Fusco

INVOLTINI DI TONNO

Fillet of Tuna Roll

INGREDIENTS

11 large tuna fillets

¼ cup oil

½ cup yellow onion minced

4 clove garlic chopped

1 pound tomatoes, peeled and chopped

4 cloves of garlic, peeled and chopped

1 slice Italian bread firm, crumbled

¼ cup milk

1 egg, beaten

1 hard boiled egg

¼ cup chopped parsley

¼ cup grated Romano cheese

DIRECTIONS

In a skillet heat oil, add onion and cook for 1 minute, add garlic and sauté until golden, then add tomatoes, a pinch of salt and ground black pepper. Cook for 20 minutes on low heat.

Soak bread into milk for 5 minutes and squeeze with your hand to dry out the bread and make it into breadcrumbs.

Wash and dry filets, and cut 1 filet into 1-inch pieces. In a bowl add soft bread, cut fish, and remaining ingredients; leave out half the parsley for garnish. Mix well. On a large work surface, lay the filets out flat and spoon the mixture over them evenly.

284

Roll up filets and secure the ends with a toothpick; add fish into tomato sauce. Cover and cook for 10 minutes on low heat. Transfer fish onto a serving platter, spoon the sauce over the rolls and serve hot.

If you want to make linguine pasta for a side dish, double the tomatoes and the oil, and cook 1 pound of pasta according to package directions. Serve hot.

Makes 5 servings.

<Buon Appetito! Emilia>

POLLO PICCATA

Chicken Piccata

INGREDIENTS

6 boneless, skinless chicken breasts cut in half

½ cup flour

½ teaspoon salt

½ teaspoon ground black pepper

2 tablespoons butter

3 cloves of garlic, peeled and chopped

¾ cup yellow onion, chopped

½ cup dry white wine

2 hot chili peppers, chopped

2 tablespoons lemon juice

1 tablespoon lemon zest

½ cup vegetable broth or water (if needed to thin sauce)

½ cup capers, packed in oil and drained

1 lemon, sliced into thin "wheels"

½ cup fresh parsley, chopped

DIRECTIONS

Combine flour, half the salt and half the black pepper in a small bowl. Coat chicken breasts with flour mixture and set aside. Save the left over flour.

In a large skillet melt ½ of the butter, add the chicken and sauté on medium heat for about 5 minutes on each side, or until chicken is no longer pink. Transfer to a large serving platter and cover with foil paper to keep warm.

In the same skillet sauté garlic and onions until golden, then add wine, chili peppers, lemon zest, lemon juice, remaining salt and black pepper. Bring to a boil and whisk in the remaining flour mixture. Simmer for 2 minutes. Whisk in the rest of the butter and pour the gravy over the chicken. Serve hot. Garnish dish with lemon slices, capers and fresh chopped parsley.

Makes 6 servings.

<Buon Appetito! Emilia>

CONGHIGLIE RIPIENE AL SALMONE

Pasta Shells Stuffed with Ricotta Cheese & Salmon

INGREDIENTS

16 pasta shells

1 tablespoon olive oil

1 cloves of garlic, peeled and chopped

1 cup tomatoes, peeled, seeded and chopped

1 pound ricotta cheese

3 oz. smoked salmon

1 egg white

½ teaspoon salt

½ teaspoon ground black pepper

DIRECTIONS

Preheat oven to 400 F.

Cook pasta shells in salt boiling water according to package directions: drain and set aside.

In a small skillet heat oil and sauté garlic until golden. Add tomatoes, a pinch of salt and black pepper. Cook for 5 minutes and then set aside.

In a blender, mix the ricotta and salmon until are a soft and creamy filling. Transfer mixture into a bowl. Whisk the egg white until fluffy and standing in soft peaks.

Mix egg white and ricotta mixture together with a wooden spatula. Stuff the shells with the mixture and cover the top with the cooked tomatoes.

Grease a baking pan with vegetable spray and put pasta shells into baking pan. Bake for 20 minutes. Serve hot.

Makes 4 servings.

<Buon Appetito! Emilia>

SPEZZATINO DI VITELLA

Veal Stew with Potatoes

INGREDIENTS

2 pounds veal stew meat

2 cloves of garlic, peeled and chopped

½ cup yellow onion, chopped

1-½ cups crushed tomatoes

1 cup dry white wine

3 basil leaves

2 bay leaves

¼ teaspoon ground black pepper

1 teaspoon salt

1 hot chili pepper

1 pound potatoes, peeled and cut in cubes

DIRECTIONS

Heat oil in a large saucepan, add veal and sauté until brown then add chopped garlic and onion and sauté for 1 minute. Add all remaining ingredients except the potatoes. Bring to a boil, then cover and simmer for 20 minutes. Add potatoes and cover and simmer for an additional 20 minutes, or until meat and potatoes are tender.

Add ½ cup water if you need more liquid. Taste for seasoning before serving, and if you think the stew is too thin, add 1 tablespoon of flour, which will thicken the stew.

Makes 6 good servings.

<Enjoy! Emilia>

FILETTE DI PESCE CON SALSA PRIMAVERA

Fish Filets with Primavera Sauce

INGREDIENTS

6 fresh fish fillets, about 6 oz each

¾ cup corn flour

2 tablespoons butter

½ teaspoon salt

½ teaspoon ground black pepper

2 tablespoons lemon juice

2 tablespoons oil

4 cloves of garlic, peeled and chopped

1 cup zucchini, cut lengthwise

1 cup fresh mushrooms, sliced

1cup cauliflower florets

1cup fresh broccoli florets

3 small bell peppers, yellow, green and red, seeded and cut into 1 inch pieces

1 tablespoon basil leaves, chopped

2 tablespoons lemon zest

DIRECTIONS

Preheat oven to 400 F.

Coat filets with corn flour, and place them in a large baking dish that has half of the butter melted in the bottom, or you can use vegetable spray. Squeeze the lemon juice over the filets, add salt and pepper bake for 4 minutes on each side, and then remove from the oven.

Meanwhile, heat oil in a large skillet, add garlic and sauté until golden. Add all remaining ingredients. Cook and stir constantly until the vegetables are tender, about 6 minutes. Spoon the vegetables over the fish filets and bake for 8 minutes.

Garnish with lemon zest, and serve hot. I never like to add cheese on a fish dish, but if you like, sprinkle 2 tablespoons of Parmesan cheese over the finished dish.

<Buon Appetito! Emilia>

ARROSTO DI MAIALE AL LATTE

Pork Tenderloin Roasted in Milk

INGREDIENTS

3 pound tenderloin pork roast

½ teaspoon salt

½ teaspoon ground black pepper

½ teaspoon rosemary flakes

½ teaspoon sage, chopped

1½ cup milk

DIRECTIONS

Butterfly your roast. Mix all the ingredients except the milk, put them inside the roast, and tie it back together with string.

In a saucepan add the milk, the roast and a pinch of salt. Bring to boiling, and then lower the heat. Cover and cook on low heat, about 25 minutes on each side, until you have about ½ cup of milk left in the saucepan. If the roast is too dry, add another ½ cup milk to the saucepan.

You need ½ cup to remain in the pan. Transfer pork to a serving platter; cut the strings and slice ½ inch thick. Pour remaining sauce over the sliced roast. Decorate with chopped parsley. Serve with a green garden salad.

Makes 6 servings.

<Buon Appetito! Emilia>

VITELLO TONNATO

Veal Roast with Tuna

INGREDIENTS

3 pound veal roast

8 oz. fresh tuna

½ cup onion, minced

2 anchovies packed in oil, chopped

1 ½ cup white wine

1 teaspoon salt

½ teaspoon ground black pepper

2 tablespoons lemon zest

½ cup capers packed in oil

2 tablespoons butter

¼ cup Italian parsley, chopped

2 lemons sliced for garnish

DIRECTIONS

Preheat oven to 375 F.

In an ovenproof skillet heat oil and sauté veal roast until brown. Add tuna, onion, anchovies, 1 cup white wine, and half the salt and black pepper. Cover and transfer the skillet into the preheated oven for 30 minutes or until the meat is tender. (Veal needs less time to cook than pork or beef.) When the roast is done, transfer to a cutting board and cover with foil to keep warm.

In the same skillet add ½ cup of the white wine and scrape down the bottom of the skillet with a wood spatula to dissolve the solids.

Simmer for 5 minutes, and if you need more liquid, add ½ cup wine or chicken stock. Then add the lemon zest, taste for salt and pepper and add if needed.

Cut the roast into ½ inch slices and arrange onto a large oval dish. Spoon the remaining juices over the roast. Garnish with chopped parsley and capers. Arrange the lemon sliced around the edge of the platter. This is a good presentation, and people like lemon over fish. Serve with baked potatoes.

Makes 6 servings

<Buon Appetito! Emilia>

PESCE SPADA FRITTO

Fried Swordfish

INGREDIENTS

2 ½ pounds swordfish cut into 3 x 2 inch pieces

2 tablespoons lemon juice

¼ teaspoon salt

½ teaspoon ground black pepper

2 tablespoons Italian parsley, chopped

3 tablespoons olive oil

2 eggs, beaten

1 cup flour

2 cups vegetable oil

DIRECTIONS

In a small bowl mix lemon, salt and black pepper, parsley and olive oil. Wash and dry swordfish and put in a shallow dish. Rub the fish with the marinade mixture and refrigerated for two hours. Then dip swordfish into eggs, then into flour on each side.

Heat vegetable oil in a large skillet and add as many swordfish pieces as will fit into the skillet. Fry until golden light brown on each side. Transfer to a dish covered with paper towels to dry the excess oil. Serve with green salad.

Makes 6 servings.

<Buon Appetito! Emilia>

INVOLTINI THE TACHHINO

Turkey Roll-up

INGREDIENTS

12 slices of turkey, 3 oz. each

3 cups chicken broth

3-½ oz. Arborio rice

1 tablespoon olive oil

2 cloves of garlic, peeled and chopped

1 pound baby spinach

2 oz. ricotta cheese

¼ cup cooked peas

1 oz. prosciutto

2 tablespoons butter

¾ cup dry white wine

1 tablespoon flour

DIRECTIONS

Add chicken broth to a saucepan and bring to a boil, then add rice and cook according to package directions. Drain rice and leave in the colander to drain well. Wash spinach. Heat the oil in a small skillet and sauté garlic until golden, then add spinach, a pinch of salt and sauté until tender. Drain the excess liquid from spinach and chop into small pieces.

Mix rice, peas, spinach and ricotta cheese; cut prosciutto in ¼ inch pieces and add to the mixture. Lay turkey slices over a flat dish, divide mixture evenly between the pieces, and then roll tight. Secure with toothpicks. Heat butter in a skillet and sauté turkey rolls until golden and brown, then add ¾ cup dry white wine.

Cover and cook at a low simmer for 20 minutes. Take turkey out the skillet, put on an oval or round flat serving dish and cover with foil to keep warm.

Add flour to the skillet and keep stirring until the broth has thickened.

Take toothpicks out of the turkey, slice diagonally and pour gravy over the meal. Serve with steamed broccoli or sautéed zucchini. Serve hot.

Makes 6 servings.

<Enjoy! Emilia >

FETTE DI VITELLA AL LIMONE & SALVIA

Veal Scaloppini with Lemon & Sage

INGREDIENTS

12 large thin slices of veal

1 cup flour

2 tablespoons butter

2 cloves of garlic, peeled and sliced

½ cup vegetable stock

½ cup white wine

1 teaspoon salt

½ teaspoon ground black pepper

2 tablespoons lemon zest

12 thin slices lemon for garnish

12 large sage leaves for garnish

DIRECTIONS

Flour each side of the veal. In a skillet heat butter and sauté veal until golden brown. Transfer to a platter, and then add chopped garlic to the skillet and sauté until golden.

Add stock and wine to the skillet, salt and black pepper; simmer until juice is about ½ cup. Add the lemon zest to skillet and veal, cook for 5 minutes.

Garnish with sliced lemon and fresh sage. Serve hot with a dish of long grain rice and steamed carrots.

Makes 6 servings.

<Buon Appetito! Emilia>

VITELLA CON CAPPERI AND ALICE

Veal with Capers & Anchovies

INGREDIENTS

8 slices veal, about 3 oz. each

1 cup flour

2 tablespoons butter

1 tablespoon balsamic vinegar

2 oz. Italian pancetta or bacon, cut ½ inch thick

4 anchovies filets

2 tablespoons capers preserved in oil

1 teaspoon salt

½ teaspoon ground black pepper

¼ cup green scallions, minced

DIRECTIONS

Coat sliced veal with the flour. In large skillet heat butter, add balsamic vinegar, then add veal and sauté each side until golden brown. Transfer veal to a dish and cover with foil to keep warm. In the same skillet, sauté pancetta until brown, and then add anchovies, capers, black pepper and a pinch of salt.

Sauté for 2 minutes, then add veal and let sauté for 1 minute longer. Transfer veal to a serving platter. Garnish with scallions and serve hot with a dish of spaghetti or a green salad.

Makes 4 servings.

<Have fun! Emilia>

TONNO DI CONIGLIO

Rabbit Tuna

INGREDIENTS

1 rabbit, about 2 to 3 pounds

2 large carrots, cut into large pieces

½ cup celery, chopped

1 yellow onion cut in half

2 bay leaves

1 small bunch of rosemary leaves

12 sage leaves

1 teaspoon salt

½ teaspoon ground black pepper

¾ cup olive oil

8 cloves of garlic, peeled and sliced in half

2 tablespoons parsley, chopped

DIRECTIONS

In a large saucepan add all the vegetables, herbs, salt and pepper. Cut rabbit in half and add to the saucepan. Bring to a boil, cover and let cook at low heat for 45 minutes or until meat is tender. Let rabbit cool off in the same pot. Take meat off the bone and shred.

In a serving dish add a little oil to the bottom and layer rabbit meat, 4 half cloves of garlic, 4 sage leaves and 3 tablespoons oil. Repeat and layer until you reach the top of the dish and/or run out of rabbit. Cover and refrigerate for one day before serving.

Before bringing the dish to the table, garnish with chopped parsley. Serve as antipasto next to Italian vinegar and a mixed vegetable dish.

<Buon Appetito! Emilia>

POLLO SEMPLICE IN PADELLA

Easy Skillet Chicken

INGREDIENTS

4 boneless chicken breast halves

2 tablespoons butter

1 tablespoon oil

2 cloves of garlic, peeled and chopped

1 teaspoon salt

½ teaspoon ground black pepper

DIRECTIONS

Wash chicken, and heat butter and oil in a medium skillet. Sauté chicken on each side until golden, and then add chopped garlic, salt and black pepper. If chicken is too dry and the bottom of the skillet is to dark, add ½ cup white dry wine to deglaze and cook for 4 minutes.

Serve with long grain rice or green salad.

Makes 4 servings.

<Buon Appetito! Emilia>

EMILIA PIATTO UNICO

Emilia's One-dish Meal

INGREDIENTS

3 tablespoons olive oil

1 cup yellow onion, minced

2 cups escarole, washed and cut

1 teaspoon salt

1 15 oz. can Italian peeled tomatoes

1 pound dry hot Italian sausage, cut into ½ inch round rings

3 large potatoes, cooked, peeled and diced

½ teaspoon ground black pepper

1 28 oz. can of burlotta or Roman beans

DIRECTIONS

Heat oil in a large skillet and sauté onion until golden. Add escarole and salt, then cover and cook on low to steam the greens for 5 minutes. Add tomatoes and sliced sausage and cook for 5 minutes, then add diced potatoes and black pepper. Cook for an additional 5 minutes.

If the mixture is to dry, add 1 cup of water or 1 cup chicken broth. Add beans and cook on low heat for 2 minutes. Serve hot with bruschetta or rosemary breadsticks.

Makes 6 to 8 servings.

<Buon Appetito!>

BRACIOLE DI CARNE DI MANZO

Stuffed-thin Steak

INGREDIENTS

2 pounds round steak, 1 pound each, cut ½ inch thick

½ cup Romano cheese, grated

4 cloves of garlic, peeled and minced

½ teaspoon ground black pepper

1 teaspoon salt

1 tablespoons olive oil

DIRECTIONS

Lay steaks flat and brush with olive oil, spread the Romano evenly and sprinkle with garlic, parsley, salt and black pepper. Gently roll steaks like a log. Tie with string to hold the shape.

Heat oil and sauté the braciola until brown on all sides. From here there are two ways to finish the braciola:

If you want to serve without sauce: After you sauté the braciola, put them into a baking dish with 1 cup dry white wine, 2 cloves of garlic peeled and sliced, 1 small bunch of rosemary and bake in a preheated oven at 375 F. for 20 to 30 minutes.

If you want to serve with sauce: add 4 cups of marinara sauce to the saucepan and simmer for 30 to 40 minutes or until meat is tender. When meat is done, transfer to a serving dish, cut string and slice braciola ½ inch thick slice and drizzle a little sauce over the sliced rolls.

Serve as a side dish or as a main dish with steamed broccoli rapi or green beans.

<Have fun! Emilia>

CARNE DI MAIALE E POLLO ALLA GRIGLIA

Grilled Pork & Chicken

INGREDIENTS

12 bamboo skewers

1 pound of pork fillets

1 pound boneless chicken breasts

4 cloves of garlic, peeled and minced

½ teaspoon brown sugar

4 tablespoons soy sauce

2 tablespoons olive oil

DIRECTIONS

Soak bamboo skewers in water before use, as this will prevent the bamboo from burning.

Cut pork and chicken into 1½ inch cubes. Combine all remaining ingredients in a bowl, add meat, stir to coat evenly and let marinate for 1 hour.

Preheat oven to broil. Thread cubes of meats onto bamboo skewers and arrange skewers on grill pan. Cook in preheated oven for 8 minutes, turning once at the 4-minute mark.

Serve warm with a dish of rice and snow peas or baked Roman beans.

Make 6 servings.

<Have fun! Emilia>

POLLO CON ACETO BALSAMIC AL ROSAMARINO

Balsamic Rosemary Chicken

INGREDIENTS

4 boneless chicken breast halves

3 tablespoons balsamic vinegar

1 teaspoon mustard

1 tablespoon fresh rosemary, minced (or dry)

2 cloves of garlic, peeled and minced

DIRECTIONS

Preheat oven to 400 F.

Combine vinegar, mustard, rosemary and garlic in a plastic bag. Add chicken, then seal and rotate bag until marinade is combined and chicken is evenly coated. Put bag into refrigerator and let marinate for 1 hour.

Arrange chicken in a baking dish and bake for 15 minutes. Slice and serve over a mixed green salad.

<Enjoy! Emilia>

SALSICCIE E SAN. NICOLA PEPERONI AL FORNO

Baked Saint Nicolas Peppers and Italian Sausage

INGREDIENTS

6 San. Nicolas peppers, green and red, cored

1 cup peeled tomatoes, seeded and chopped

4 cloves of garlic, peeled and chopped

1 cup red onions and white, sliced ½ inch thin

2 red chili peppers, chopped

1 teaspoon salt

3 tablespoons extra virgin olive oil

6 hot Italian pork sausage links

DIRECTIONS

Preheat oven to 400 F.

Mix all vegetables in a large bowl with 2 tablespoons of oil and the salt. Transfer to a large roasting pan and bake for 5 minutes.

While the vegetables are roasting, add 1 tablespoon of the oil to a nonstick skillet and sauté sausage until brown, about 8 minutes.

Remove pan from oven and add sausage and then chopped tomatoes over the vegetables. Reduce heat to 375 F. bake for 10 more minutes, or until the sausage links are cooked through.

Serve over cooked rice or your favorite pasta.

<Buon Appetito! Emilia>

SCAMPI ALLA GRIGLIA PICCANTE

Spicy Grilled Shrimp

INGREDIENTS

3 cups cooked brown rice

4 pounds jumbo shrimp

4 cloves of garlic, peeled and chopped

¼ cup fresh Italian parsley, chopped

1 tablespoon tarragon, chopped

2 red chili peppers, chopped

1 teaspoon fresh squeezed lemon juice

3 teaspoons extra virgin olive oil

¼ cup dry white wine

½ teaspoon salt

½ teaspoon fresh ground pepper

DIRECTIONS

Wash shrimp, split them in the middle, and take the vein out of the center of the back. In a large bowl mix ½ of the chopped garlic, ½ of the chopped parsley, tarragon, ½ salt and black pepper, chili peppers, 1 teaspoon olive oil, the white wine and lemon juice. Mix well, toss shrimp into the mixture, cover with plastic wrap and marinate for 2 hours in the refrigerator.

You can either grill the shrimp, or place them in a broiler pan, brush remaining marinade juice over shrimp and broil until shrimp turn pink. This takes a very short amount of time, and you should turn the shrimp once, so check frequently.

Meanwhile, in a small skillet add remaining oil, chopped garlic, red pepper and 2 tablespoons of water and sauté for 30 seconds. Toss shrimp into the mixture and arrange shrimp over bed of rice and sprinkle with remaining chopped parsley. Serve hot or cool.

Makes 6 servings.

<Buon Appetito! Emilia>

TONNO A MODO MIO

Tuna My Way

INGREDIENTS

½ cup extra virgin olive oil

¼ cup fresh oregano, chopped

3 cloves of garlic, peeled and chopped

½ teaspoon salt

1 teaspoon fresh ground black pepper

2 tablespoons fresh Italian parsley, chopped

6 tuna steaks, about ½ pound each

DIRECTIONS

In a bowl mix first 6 ingredients. Wash tuna and add to the bowl, turning to coat each side with the marinade mixture. Grill tuna for about 4 minutes on each side.

When tuna is done serve over a bed of green lettuce with the remaining marinade over the top of the tuna.

Makes 6 servings.

<Have fun in your kitchen! Emilia>

LINGUINETTE AL SAPORE DI MARE

Seafood Linguine

INGREDIENTS

1 pound linguine

1 box (12 oz.) frozen chopped asparagus

2 tablespoons extra virgin olive oil

2 tablespoons butter

6 cloves of garlic, peeled and thinly sliced

8 oz. bay scallops

1 cup Italian parsley, chopped

8 oz. cooked medium shrimp

1 pinch salt and ground black pepper

DIRECTIONS

In large pot of light salt boiling water, cook linguine al dente.

While the pasta is cooking, wash and snap bottom portion of the asparagus stalks and discard the ends, then heat the oil in a large skillet and sauté garlic until golden brown. Add butter and asparagus, then sauté for 2 minutes on low heat.

Add scallops, mushrooms and half the parsley, and then cook on low heat for an additional 2 minutes.

Add shrimp to the skillet, toss until they turn pink and then add linguine to the skillet. Toss linguine for 30 seconds so that all ingredients will be mixed thoroughly. Transfer linguine mixture to a serving platter, garnish with remaining parsley.

Serve when pasta is hot.

Making 6 servings.

<Buon Appetito! Emilia>

PETTO DI POLLO PIENO CON SPINACI

Spinach Stuffed Chicken Breasts

INGREDIENTS

6 boneless skinless chicken breast halves

2 tablespoons extra virgin olive oil

2 cloves of garlic, peeled and chopped

¼ cup onion, finely chopped

½ cup sweet red and green pepper, finely diced

½ teaspoon fresh rosemary, chopped

1 package (12 oz.) frozen chopped spinach, thawed and drained

¼ cup chopped Italian parsley

½ teaspoon salt

½ teaspoon fresh ground black pepper

½ cup mozzarella cheese, shredded

DIRECTIONS

Heat 1 teaspoon of oil in a medium skillet and sauté garlic until golden. Add onion, green and red peppers and sauté for 4 minutes until peppers are tender. Add spinach, half of the salt and black pepper and half the chopped rosemary. Cook for 4 minutes, and then remove from the heat, let cool and stir in shredded cheese and half the parsley.

In each chicken breast, cut a pocket through thicker side. Divide spinach mixture into 6 equal portions and fill each chicken breast, then secure the pocket with 2 toothpicks.

In a small bowl mix remaining salt, black pepper and rosemary. Rub chicken breasts on both sides. Grill (on a preheated grill) for 8 to 10 minutes each side on medium heat, or until chicken is no longer pink. Slice chicken 1 inch thick on the diagonal. Garnish with remaining parsley, and serve over a bed of fresh green salad.

This stuffing mixture can be use for pork loin, turkey breast, veal roasts and even lasagna roll-ups.

<Buon Appetito! Emilia>

FILETTO DI VITELLA ALLE AROME DI ERBE

Herbed Butterflied (boneless) Veal Chops

INGREDIENTS

6 butterflied veal chops, about 4 oz. each

Herbs:

1 teaspoon dried rosemary

½ cup fresh parsley, chopped

1 teaspoon dried sage

3 tablespoons lemon juice

½ teaspoon ground black pepper

1 teaspoon salt

DIRECTIONS

Preheat the broiler in your oven or preheat your grill.

In a small bowl combine all ingredients, leaving half of the parsley for garnish, and rub the mixture on both sides of the veal chops. Broil or grill for 6 to 7 minutes on each side.

Transfer chops to a serving platter and garnish with remaining parsley. Serve immediately with steamed asparagus, carrot spears or steamed broccoli rapi.

<Buon Appetito! Emilia>

8. DESERTS

NOCINO

Walnut Liquor

INGREDIENTS

30 walnuts

2-½ cups sugar

2-½ cups water

750-ml. Grain alcohol (95 to 100 C.)

3 whole piece cinnamon sticks

DIRECTIONS

Bring water and sugar to a boiling. When water is cool; put water into a 3 or 4 lit. gallon. Add cinnamon sticks and cover until the walnut skins are peeled.

In Southern Italy walnuts are down in October. To make the Nocino liqueur we pick the walnuts the third week of June. On the time the outside part are green, and that what we need.

Trim the green parts from the walnuts and put them into a gallon with the water. During this soaking process, the mixture should be stirred occasionally for a 40 day period.

After 40 days the mixture is filtered and passed through paper or cloth filter and then bottled. Leave Nocino to mature for at least six months.

Different from Limoncello, this is liqueur strongly aromatic and brown in color.

Because of its flavor: this is a liquor you want to drink at and of the meals.

(This liquor is for adults only. Enjoy Emilia>

LIMONCELLO

Lemon Liquors

INGREDIENTS

9 large lemons with good skin

1 bottle of vodka 750 ml or (proof or grain alcohol 95 to 100 C.)

2-½ cups water

2-¼ cups sugar

DIRECTIONS

Rinse lemons in cool water and peel skin with a potato peeler. Do not cut the white part, and keep knife away from the lemon. If you see it on the back of the yellow skin trim it off with a sharp knife.

Boil water and sugar in a large saucepan, stir until dissolved and boil for 4 minutes. Let sugar mixture cool completely in the pan before mixing with vodka and lemon skin. Pour the mixture into a gallon-size container and seal tightly.

Put gallon in a cool and dark place, perhaps in the corner of a cabinet. For

45 days (about 5 weeks), 2 to 3 times per week, shake the container upside down to mix the liquor. After the 40 days, strain the liquor into a big jar so that the lemon peel is removed and pour into a decorative bottle. Store in the freezer. (It is safe to put bottles of liquor into the freezer, as the alcohol content is so high that the liquid will not freeze and break the bottle.) Only take liquor out when you are serving it.

You can make orange and tangerine liquors with this recipe too.

<This is for adults only! Enjoy! Emilia>

GRANITA DI LIMONE E CAMPARI VERMOUTH

Lemon-Campari Granita

INGREDIENTS

1 cup sugar

¾ cup water

2 ½ cups unsweetened lemon juice

1 cup Campari Vermouth

DIRECTIONS

In a saucepan combine water and sugar, bring to a boil and remove from heat.

In a large bowl, stir together lemon juice and Campari Vermouth, and then add sugar mixture to the juice mixture. Stir well to combine, let cool to room temperature, and then transfer the mixture to any 9 by 13-inch baking pan.

Cover the pan with plastic food wrap and freeze until firm about 9 hours.

Scrape the granita with a fork to make shaved ice and spoon into individual dishes to serve.

Makes 12 servings.

<This desert is for adults only. Enjoy! Emilia>

COCKTAL DORATO

Golden Cocktail

INGREDIENTS

1 oz. strega (liquor)

1 oz. white wine

1 tablespoon sugar

1 tablespoons lemon juice

2 tablespoons crushed ice

DIRECTIONS

Add all of the ingredients into a blender. Blend for 1 minute. Fill a large glass about ¼ full with crushed ice and pour drink into glass. Garnish with a slice of lemon.

Makes 1 serving.

<This drink is for adults only! Emilia>

Emilia Fusco

COCKTAL DI MELONE AND KIWI

Cantaloupe & Kiwi Cocktail

INGREDIENTS

5 kiwi fruit

1 large ripe cantaloupe

4 cups white rum

3 cups dry white wine

3 cups champagne

DIRECTIONS

Cut the cantaloupe in half, take seeds out, cut the skin off and cut into ½ inch cubes. In a bowl mix cantaloupe and half the rum, then cover and refrigerate for 2 hours.

Pour the remaining rum into an ice cube tray and freeze.

Peel kiwis and slice very thin. Put in a bowl, add 1 ½ cup white wine, mix and refrigerate for 2 hours.

Prepare a large punch bowl 10 minutes before your company arrives. Mix all the ingredients from the refrigerator, and then add the wine and champagne.

Just before your company arrives add rum cubes to the punch bowl and serve.

Makes 12 servings.

<This cocktail is for adults only! Enjoy! Emilia>

324

TORTA DI CAMPAGNA ALLA CALABRESE

Calabrian Country Torte

INGREDIENTS

6 oz. butter

7 oz. powdered sugar

1 large lemon, zest

¼ teaspoon ground cinnamon

5 eggs, separated

2 oz. flour

4 teaspoons baking powder

1 pinch salt

DIRECTIONS

Preheat oven to 350 F.

In a medium sized bowl, cut the butter into small pieces, and then add sugar and salt. Use an electric mixer to combine until very soft, like a cream, and then add the lemon zest, the eggs yolks one at time, and the cinnamon. Sift flour and baking powder together, then add to the mixture in stages and blend well.

Beat egg whites in a separate bowl until they become large and fluffy like a snowball. Gently fold the whites into the torte using a spatula to mix them very gently.

Pour cake mixture into greased 9-inch cake pan. Bake for 40 to 50 minutes. As the cake is cooling down, sprinkle the top with powdered sugar or decorate the top with this glaze.

FOR THE GLAZE

Heat 3 tablespoons of Amaretto the Sarronno. Take off the stove, add 4 oz. of powdered sugar and blend well until it becomes a soft glaze. Spread the glaze evenly over the cake and let chill before serving.

Makes 8 servings.

<Eat half portions to cut the calories in half. Enjoy! Emilia>

TORTA AL CACAO SENSA ZUCCERO

Cocoa Cake Without Sugar

INGREDIENTS

3 cups all-purpose flour

6 tablespoons sweet (Dutch process) cocoa powder

1 tablespoon baking soda

2 tablespoons white vinegar

2 cups cool water

¼ teaspoon salt

¼ cup olive oil

DIRECTIONS

Preheat oven to 400 F.

Add all of the ingredients except the olive oil in a large bowl and combine using an electric mixer. Mix on low speed for about 2 minutes, then add oil and mix well.

Grease a 9 x 12-inch cake pan and pour the batter into the greased pan. Bake for 20 minutes, and then reduce the oven temperature to 350 F. and bake for 20 more minutes.

Transfer cake onto a cooling rack for about 10 minutes. After that, you can cut it into 2-inch squares and serve with your favorite ice cream, coffee or tea.

<Indulge yourself! Not too often Emilia>

CAPPUCCINO TIRAMISU`

Tiramisu

INGREDIENTS

3 egg yolks

½ cup sugar

1 cup espresso Italian coffee

½ cup coffee brandy

3 eggs whites

1 package plain gelatin

2 cup whipping cream

2 ½ doz. Italian biscotti (30) Italian biscotti

CHOCOLATE COVER

2 cups whipping cream

½ cup granulated sugar

¼ cup coffee espresso beans

TOPPINGS

½ cup cocoa

¼ cup chocolate covered espresso beans

DIRECTIONS

Beat 1 cup sugar and 2 cups whipping cream until fluffy and almost doubled in volume. Add the eggs yolks one at a time, and then mix in gelatin and coffee brandy. Refrigerate until the cream is firm, and save about ½ cup for decoration. Beat egg whites with an electric mixer until stiff and fold into cream mixture.

Using a cake dish, 12 x 12. In a small bowl pour Italian espresso coffee: dip each biscuit into the coffee. Start the tiramisu with a layer of biscotti, then one layer of cream mixture until you reach the top of the dish, finishing with a layer of the cream mixture.

Pour the ½ cup of reserved cream mixture into a piping bag. Sift cocoa over the top and then decorate with small roses and sprinkle the top with the espresso beans. Refrigerate at least 2 hours before serving.

Makes 10 servings.

<Enjoy! Emilia>

TORTA ALLE MELE E NOCE

Apple & Walnut Cake

INGREDIENTS

2 teaspoons butter

5 apples, peeled and finely chopped

1 ½ cups walnuts, chopped

3 ½ cups all-purpose flour

1 ¾ cup granulated sugar

¼ cup brown sugar

1 cup vegetable oil

2 eggs, beaten

1 tablespoon baking soda

½ teaspoon salt

½ teaspoon ground nutmeg

1 teaspoon vanilla extract

½ teaspoon ground cinnamon

DIRECTIONS

Preheat oven to 375 F.

Melt butter in a non-stick pan and cook apples until tender. Be careful, because if you cook the apples too long the cake will be soggy. Transfer the apples to a bowl with both sugars. Let stand for 15 minutes, stirring often, to allow mixture to make juice, and then add eggs, oil, and vanilla to the apples.

In a separate bowl, combine the flour, baking soda, cinnamon, salt, nutmeg, and walnuts, then add to the apple mixture and combine thoroughly.

Grease a 10-inch tube pan or fluted pan and pour the cake mixture into the pan. Bake for 50 minutes, or until a wooden toothpick inserted in the center comes out clean. Cool pan on wire rack for 10 minutes, and then remove cake from pan and cool completely on rack before serving.

If you like a little spice, add 1 tablespoon of cognac when cooking the apples at first.

<Serve with your favorite ice scream. Enjoy! Emilia>

NO MASCARPONE TIRAMISU

Tiramisú Without Mascarpone

INGREDIENTS

1 ½ cups (12 oz.) ricotta cheese

10 oz. cream cheese

1 cup powdered sugar

1 package of ladyfingers

½ cup espresso coffee

½ cup coffee brandy

2 cups heavy cream, whipped

2 tablespoons cocoa powder

1 teaspoon cinnamon

DIRECTIONS

Let the ricotta cheese drain for 1 hour over the sink in a piece of cheesecloth or a very fine sieve.

Mix ricotta, cream cheese and powdered sugar with an electric hand mixer until all ingredients are well combined.

In a small bowl, mix coffee brandy and espresso coffee and soak the ladyfingers for a few seconds each. Then line the bottom of a 12-inch round cake dish with about half of the soaked ladyfingers.

(Use a glass dish if you want a nice presentation.)

Pour about half of the cheese mixture over the ladyfingers and then layer on the second half of the ladyfingers. Cover the ladyfingers with the second half of the cheese mixture and then top with whipped cream.

Combine cocoa and cinnamon and sift over the top. Chill overnight.

Cut into small slices as you would cut a cake. Tiramisú can be decorated with espresso coffee beans!

<Don't eat a big slice! Emilia>

TORTA ALL'ARANCIO

Orange Cake

INGREDIENTS

2 cups sugar

2 sticks butter

4 eggs, separated

2 oranges, zest and juiced

2½ cups all-purpose flour

4 teaspoons baking powder

¼ cup milk

DIRECTIONS

Preheat oven to 375 F.

In a large bowl, mix together butter and sugar until light and fluffy. Using an electric hand mixer, add egg yolks one at a time, mixing well after each addition. Then add orange juice and mix until well combined.

In a separate bowl, sift together flour, salt and baking powder. With a wooden spatula fold the dry ingredients into the cream mixture as lightly as possible, and then stir in the orange zest.

In a separate bowl, whisk eggs whites until they reach the soft peak stage, and then fold them into the mixture. Pour cake mix into a greased and floured round cake pan and bake for 45 minutes.

Insert a thin piece of spaghetti into center of the cake. If it comes out moist, then the cake needs to bake for a few more minutes. If the spaghetti is dry, then take cake out of oven let cool for 5 minutes.

Let cool completely on a rack before frosting.

FROSTING

1 can evaporated milk

¾ cup sugar

1 stick butter

Mix all the ingredients in a pan and cook, stirring over medium heat, until mixture has an even consistency. . Let cool completely before frosting cake. If you choose to add crème (recipe is on the next page), cut the cake in half (parallel to the counter) and add crème in the middle of cake. Then assemble the cake and frost it.

<Have fun! Emilia>

PER LA CRÈME PASTICCIERA

Crème Filling for Cakes

INGREDIENTS

2 cups milk

6 eggs yolks

1 cup sugar

6 tablespoons flour

1 pinch salt

½ teaspoon vanilla

DIRECTIONS

In a nonstick saucepan, add milk and heat on medium.

Beat egg yolks and sugar together until well combined. Add flour, salt and vanilla to the egg mixture, and when the milk is almost boiling, slowly add ¼ cup hot milk to the egg mixture.

Mix well and then add remaining milk to the egg mixture and stir with a whisk constantly until thick enough to spread.

Let crème cool completely before using in deserts.

<Enjoy! Emilia>

TORTA AL ROOM

Rum Cake

INGREDIENTS

6 eggs, separated

1 ¼ cup sugar

½ cup milk

2 tablespoons rum extract

1 lemon, zest and juiced

½ cup extra virgin olive oil

4 cups flour

6 teaspoons baking powder

1 teaspoon vanilla powder

DIRECTIONS

Preheat oven to 400 F.

With electric mixer, beat yolks and sugar together, and then add milk, rum, lemon juice, lemon zest and oil. Mix thoroughly.

In a separate bowl, sift flour, baking powder and vanilla powder together. Add flour to the egg mixture 1 cup at time, mixing well between additions of flour.

In a separate bowl, beat egg whites for 2 minutes, and then fold into cake mixture with a spatula by hand.

Grease and flour a bunt cake pan and bake for 30 minutes, then lower the heat to 350 F. and bake for 25 more minutes. Let cake cool for 10 minutes, then transfer to a serving platter and decorate with vanilla sugar. Serve with your favorite ice cream. (Thank you Maria Iafrate)

<Indulge yourself with a small slice! Emilia>

PANNA COTTA

Italian Custard

INGREDIENTS

½ cup sugar

3½ teaspoons unflavored gelatin

3 cups whipping cream

3 cups buttermilk

1 cup fresh chopped fruit from season

½ cup toasted pine nuts

DIRECTIONS

In a medium saucepan, combine sugar and gelatin and add cream. Heat and stir until gelatin is dissolved. Remove from heat and stir in the buttermilk.

Pour panna into 12 individual custard cups, cover and chili for 6 to 12 hours, or until set.

To serve, immerse bottom of the cups into hot water: run a clean knife around edge to loosen. Invert into dessert plate. Serve with fresh fruit and toasted pine nuts.

<Have fun! Emilia>

TORTA DI RICOTTA

Ricotta Pie

INGREDIENTS

1 package frozen pastry dough

2 pounds fresh ricotta cheese

3 egg yolks

2 whole eggs

1 tablespoon rum

1 oz. slivered almonds

½ cup sugar

DIRECTIONS

Preheat oven to 400 F.

Use a piece of cheesecloth to squeeze all of the excess liquid out of the ricotta and set aside in a colander or sieve to let drain until ready to use.

Grease a 9-inch spring-form cake pan, roll out one piece of pastry dough and cover the bottom of the pan. Then roll out the second piece and cut into ¾ inch strips to decorate the top of the cake in a lattice pattern. (A pizza cutter works well for this job.)

Using a hand mixer, beat eggs and sugar for 2 minutes, then add ricotta cheese and rum by hand with a spatula. Fill cake pan with the ricotta mixture and top with the pastry strips in a lattice pattern.

Bake for 30 minutes, and then reduce the heat to 375 F. and bake for an additional 40 minutes.

Insert a piece of thin spaghetti through the center of the cake. If the spaghetti is clear, that means the cake is done. If there is ricotta sticking to the spaghetti, bake for 5-10 minutes longer.

Decorate top of the cake with almonds and powdered sugar. If you want to make this cake very fancy, leave off the almonds and add your favorite fresh fruit to the top before sprinkling with powdered sugar.

<Indulge yourself with thin slice! Emilia>

TORTA DI RICOTTA E AL YOGURT

Ricotta Pie with Yogurt

INGREDIENTS

4 eggs

1 pound ricotta cheese

½ cup sugar

½ cup all-purpose flour, sifted

2 plain yogurt cups

1 tablespoon white rum

2 tablespoons lemon zest

½ cup skim milk

1 pinch salt

¼ cup confectioners' sugar

DIRECTIONS

Preheat oven to 375 F.

In a large bowl, beat eggs with hand electric mixer then add sugar and mix well. Add yogurt, milk, ricotta, rum and lemon zest.

Sifted flour, confection sugar and salt: mix well, and then with wood spatula fold in the dry ingredients until the mixture is very smooth.

Grease and flour a 9-inch round springform cake pan.

Add mixture into pan and bake for 50 minutes. Check after 30 minutes, and if the top is turning too brown, cover with foil. Let pie cool down before sprinkling powdered sugar over the top.

Makes 8 servings.

<Enjoy! Emilia>

SOUFFLÉ AL LIMONE

Lemon Soufflé

INGREDIENTS

1 cup milk

1 teaspoon lemon or plain gelatin

2 eggs, separated

2 lemons, juiced

3 tablespoons sugar

DIRECTIONS

In small saucepan heat milk, add 1 piece of lemon rind and the gelatin. Stir constantly, and as soon as the milk is warm, take it off of the stove and discard the lemon skin.

In the bottom of a double boiler add 3 cups water and bring to a boil. While the water is heating, add sugar and egg yolks to the top pan of the double boiler and beat well until fluffy. Once water is boiling, place top pan on the boiler and keep whisking until eggs and sugar are very thick.

Take off the heat and let cool, and then add the eggs to the milk mixture.

Beat 1 egg white until light and fluffy. With wooden spoon fold the egg white into the mixture and then pour into 4-soufflé dishes.

Cover the outside of the dishes with foil that comes to about ½ inch over the top. Transfer soufflé into the freezer until it is firm. Remove from the freezer 30 minutes before serving.

Makes 4 servings.

<Enjoy! Emilia>

TARALLUCCI CADDI E FRIDDI

Ciambelle Hot & Cold

INGREDIENTS

2 eggs

2 tablespoons sugar

2 tablespoons rum

½ teaspoon cinnamon

1 pinch vanilla powder

1 cup all-purpose flour

1 ½ cup vegetable oil for frying

DIRECTIONS

Beat the first 5 ingredients together in a medium sized bowl, then add flour half cup at time and work the dough until it has a good elastic consistency, like when you make bread.

Roll dough to the thickness of ziti pasta and 5 inches long. Tie ends together to form a small knot or circle. Put all the ciambelletti on the table over a tablecloth. In skillet heat oil, wan oil is very: hot added ciambelletti 4 or 5 at time depending on the size of the fry skillet.

Turn while frying so that they are golden brown on all sides. Cover a big dish with paper towels so that when you remove the ciambelletti from the oil, they will dry off the excess oil.

Sprinkle with powdered sugar for a nice presentation.

<Indulge yourself! Emilia>

TORTA PAZZA

Wacky Cake

INGREDIENTS

3 cups sifted flour

2 cups sugar

1 tablespoon cocoa powder

2 tablespoons baking soda

1 tablespoon salt

2/3 cup extra virgin olive oil

2 tablespoons vinegar

2 tablespoons vanilla

2 cups cold water

DIRECTIONS

Preheat oven to 350 F.

Mix all of the dry ingredients with a wooden spatula. Make 3 holes in the mixture. In the first put the extra virgin olive oil, in the second, the vinegar, and in the third the vanilla.

Add 2 cups of cold water and mix thoroughly. Grease a large cake pan (9x13) and bake for 40 to 45 minutes. When cake has cooled down, frost or serve with whipped cream.

<Indulge yourself with thin slice! Emilia>

TORTA DI FOR MAGGIO

Crushed Graham Cracker Cheesecake

CRUST INGREDIENTS

½ cup sugar

2 cups crushed graham crackers

¼ cup butter or margarine melted

FILLING INGREDIENTS

3 packages (8 oz. each) cream cheese

3 eggs

½ teaspoon vanilla powder

½ cup sugar

DIRECTIONS

Preheat oven to 350 F.

Mix the first 3 ingredients, press into bottom of a spring form pan and put in the refrigerator.

Make sure cream cheese is very soft and the eggs are at room temperature. Mix all of the filling ingredients with an electric hand mixer at low speed until well combined and pour into the pan with the prepared crust.

Bake for 40 minutes. Let cake cool and refrigerate for 4 hours before serving.

<Have fun! Emilia>

TORTA ALLA MOCA

Mocha Cake

INGREDIENTS

4 eggs, separated

¼ cup water

½ cup sugar

2 tablespoons espresso coffee

4 tablespoons cocoa

1 cup all-purpose flour

2 tablespoons baking powder

FROSTING

1 cup confectioner sugar

¼ cup heavy cream

1 tablespoon butter

1 tablespoon coffee brandy

DIRECTIONS

Preheat oven to 350 F.

With an electric mixer beat egg yolks, water, sugar and espresso coffee, and then add cocoa powder, flour and baking powder.

In a separate bowl beat egg whites until stiff, and then fold into flour mixture with a wooden spatula. Grease two 8-inch round spring form cake pans and add a wax paper lining on the bottom.

Bake for 20 minutes or until a piece of spaghetti inserted in the center comes out clean. Transfer cake to a rack to cool.

FROSTING

Mix all frosting ingredients with an electric mixer until stiff and smooth.

Put one cake on a serving plate; spread frosting over entire cake, top with the second cake and cover entire cake. Refrigerate cake for at least 4 hours before serving.

<Have fun! Emilia>

CIAMBELLA A MODO MIO SEMPLICE

Emilia's Easy Cake

INGREDIENTS

2 eggs

1 ½ cups sugar

1 teaspoon liquid extract vanilla

1¾ cup flour

½ cup melted butter

½ cup warm milk

2 tablespoons baking powder

¼ cup olive oil

½ cup almonds, finely chopped

1 pinch salt

½ cup almonds, very thinly sliced

DIRECTIONS

Preheat oven to 375 F.

Use an electric mixer to beat eggs well. Add sugar and vanilla and beat for 1 minute more, until you have soft yellow cream. Add butter and warm milk, then add oil and mix well.

Add flour, baking powder and chopped almonds and beat for 1 minute.

Grease a round cake pan; pour in the batter and bake for 40 minutes.

When cake is done, transfer to a serving dish and garnish top with sliced almonds. Serve with coffee or your favorite drinks.

Makes 8 to 10 servings.

<Enjoy! Emilia>

SALAME DI CIOCCOLATO

Chocolate Salami

INGREDIENTS

1 cup butter, softened

¾ cup sugar

4 egg yolks

½ cup unsweetened cocoa

½ almonds, finely chopped

½ cup rum

2-½ cup ladyfingers cookies, crumbled

½ cup amaretti cookies, crushed

DIRECTIONS

Mix butter and half the sugar in one bowl. In another bowl, beat the egg yolks and remaining sugar, then combine the mixes.

Sift cocoa powder and chopped almonds into the mixture, and then add rum and crumbled cookies. Mix well.

Roll the mixture into a salami shape. Wrap in foil and roll again so that the "salami" is evenly rounded. Tie roll together at the ends to keep roll round and closed.

Put the chocolate roll into the refrigerator for 3 hours before cutting. Cut into ½ inch rounds for serving.

<Enjoy! Emilia>

TORTA AL LIMONE E RICOTTA

Lemon Cheesecake

INGREDIENTS

1 ½ cup ricotta cheese

1 ½ cup sugar

4 eggs, divided

2 tablespoons liquor strega or Galliano

3 cups flour, sifted

Zest from 3 lemons

1 stick butter, softened to room temperature

1 egg, beaten

¼ teaspoon salt

DIRECTIONS

Preheat oven to 375 F. when ready to bake.

Sift flour and salt, and then cut the softened butter into the mix. Work through until the dough is very smooth. Wrap the mixture in plastic wrap and refrigerate for 2 hours. While waiting, drain ricotta with cheesecloth for 20 minutes. Mix ricotta cheese, lemon zest, sugar and the four eggs yolks.

Beat the egg whites until fluffy and stiff, then with a wooden or plastic spatula, gently fold egg whites into ricotta mixture. Divide dough into 2 portions and roll each to a one-inch thickness. Grease a 9-inch spring form cake pan all round and place one of the dough sheets in the bottom of the pan. Put ricotta mixture into the pan and use a pizza cutter or decorated (pastry) cutting wheel to cut ¾ inch strips from remaining dough.

Cover the top cake with dough strips, first vertical and then horizontal, to make a lattice pattern. Fold the side dough over the strips, as this will seal the ends. Beat the whole egg and brush over the dough strips and all round. Bake for 40 to 50 minutes. Check the cake at 30 minutes, and if it looks too dark, cover with foil. Let cake cool down before serving.

Makes 8 to 10 servings

<From my kitchen to your table. Buon Appetito! Emilia>

TORTA AL LIMONE

Lemon Cake

INGREDIENTS

7 eggs, separated

¾ cup powdered sugar

2 tablespoons of lemon zest

¼ cup lemon juice

2 cups lightly sifted all-purpose flour

1 pinch salt

DIRECTIONS

Preheat oven to 350 F.

In a large bowl beat egg yolks until thickened, add ½ the sugar and beat until thick, then add lemon zest and lemon peel, and keep beating until smooth. Add flour and salt gradually add to the yolk mixture.

In another mixing bowl beat egg whites until soft peaks form. Slowly add remaining sugar and keep beating until stiff peaks form. Gently fold the egg white mixture into the flour mixture.

Grease a 10-inch tube cake pan and bake on the lower rack for 35 minutes. Remove from the oven and immediately run a knife around sides of cake and pan. Remove cake from the pan and cool for about 45 minutes on a wire rack.

When ready to serve, put cake on a serving platter and sprinkle cake with powdered sugar. Serve with your favorite ice cream.

<Enjoy! Emilia>

BUDINO ITALIANO

Italian Pudding

INGREDIENTS

7 oz. sweetened condensed milk

2 eggs

1 oz. coffee brandy liquor

FOR THE CARAMEL

1 cup brown sugar

1 stick butter

1 pinch salt

DIRECTIONS

Preheat oven to 375 F.

Melt the butter in a small saucepan, and then add the brown sugar and salt. When the sugar is completely dissolved in the butter and has come to a caramel stage, take off of the heat and put aside.

Thoroughly combine condensed milk and eggs with an electric hand mixer, then add brandy liquor and mix well.

Pour caramel into small round baking dish and add the custard mixture over the caramel.

Put dish into a large pan with water about halfway up the sides of the pudding dish, as this pudding needs to be baked in a water bath. Bake for 30 to 40 minutes at 375 F.

Serve with vanilla ice cream and top with fruit of the season.

<Enjoy! Emilia>

TORTA AL CIOCCOLATO PER IL COMPLEANNO

Birthday Chocolate Cake

INGREDIENTS

3¾ cups all-purpose flour

1 teaspoon salt

3 tablespoons baking powder

¾ cup unsweetened cocoa powder

1½ stick unsalted butter

6 large eggs

1 cup heavy cream

2 cups granulated sugar

¾ cup milk

CREMA PER LA TORTA E LA DECORAZIONE

Filing for the Cake and Frosting

½ cup softened butter

½ cup whipping cream

1 ½ pound confectioner's sugar

½ cup coffee brandy

1 tablespoon vanilla

¼ cup cocoa powder

DIRECTIONS

Preheat oven to 350 F.

Sift together flour, salt, baking powder and cocoa.

In large bowl beat butter and eggs until creamy, and then add heavy cream and sugar. On low speed, slowly add flour mixture and alternate with the milk until the batter is smooth.

Grease three 12-inch round cake pans. Divide cake mixture into the pans and bake for 25 minutes.

While the cake is baking, make the filling. Beat together butter and whipping cream. Add powdered sugar until thickened, and then add ¾ of the coffee brandy and all of the vanilla. Remove 1 cup and set aside to use for the frosting, and chill the crème for 10 minutes.

When the cakes are cool, put one on a cake platter, add half the filling and smooth the crème with a spatula. Put the second cake over the filling and repeat with the second half of the crème. Layer the final cake on top and then start to mix the frosting.

For the frosting, beat cocoa powder and remaining coffee brandy into reserved chilled crème mixture, then cover top of cake. If you have crème left, spread it all over the cake. Refrigerate for 30 minutes before serving.

Makes 24 servings.

<Enjoy! Emilia>

TORTA DI CIOCCOLATA RICCA DI SAPORI

Rich Chocolate 3 Layer Cake

INGREDIENTS

8 eggs, separated

1 ½ cup sugar

2 cups all-purpose flour

4 tablespoons cocoa powder

1 pinch salt

½ cup melted butter

FILLING

10 oz. dark chocolate

¾ cup melted butter

1 cup powdered sugar

DIRECTIONS

Preheat oven to 350 F.

With electric mix beat egg yolks and sugar until mixture is very light and foamy. In a separate bowl, sift flour, cocoa powder and salt and then blend into yolk mixture, then add the melted butter.

In a big bowl whisk the egg whites until foamy and the whisk leaves a trail when lifted, then fold into cake mixture.

Grease three 9-inch square pans or three 3 rectangular 9 x 5 inch pans, and line the bottoms with parchment paper.

Divided cake mixtures into 3 equal portions into the pans and bake for 15 minutes or until a toothpick comes out clear from the center.

To make the filling, melt chocolate and butter together over low heat, then remove from the heat and stir in the confectioner's sugar. Let cool and then beat with an electric mixer until thick enough to spread.

When the cakes are cool, put one on a cake platter, add half the filling and smooth the filling with a spatula. Put the second cake over the filling and repeat. Layer the final cake on top and finish frosting the cake.

Sprinkle grated dark chocolate over the top, and refrigerate for 2 hours before serving. You can also decorate the sides with slivered toasted almonds or hazelnuts for an extra effect.

<Enjoy! Emilia>

EMILIA SUSUMELLI BISCOTTE

Emilia's Hazelnut Biscotti

INGREDIENTS

4 eggs

½ cup granulated sugar

16 oz. honey

2 teaspoons baking powder

1 teaspoon ground cinnamon

2 tablespoons tangerine zest

5 cups flour

½ cup extra virgin olive oil

3 cups hazelnuts, roasted

DIRECTIONS

Preheat oven at 400 F.

With electric mixer, beat eggs and sugar for 2 minutes, then add honey and beat for 2 minutes. Add baking powder, cinnamon, oil, and tangerine zest; and mix until combined.

Add flour 1 cup at a time and blend well, then add hazelnuts one cup at a time.

Divide dough into 4 portions. Sprinkle flour on a wood surface and roll each portion into 16 long by 2 inches thick long.

Cover a large biscotti (baking) pan with wax paper, space the biscotti 4 inches apart and brush with beaten eggs or milk.

Bake for 25 to 30 minutes. Slice biscotti ½ inch wide, but if you like the biscotti to have extra crunch, reduce the oven temperature to 300 F. and return them to the hot oven for 1 minute.

Biscotti can be stored in tins or a plastic container.

<Buon Appetito! Emilia>

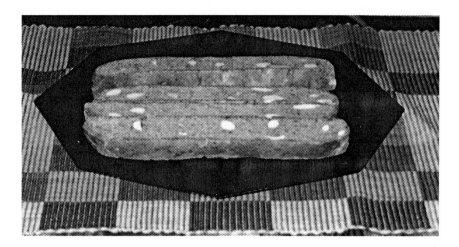

BISCOTTE ALL'ANICE

Italian Anise Cookies

INGREDIENTS

6 eggs

4 tablespoons melted shortening or butter

8 oz. confection sugar

1 tablespoon lemon extract

¼ teaspoon anise oil

6 teaspoons baking powder

3 cups flour

DIRECTIONS

Preheat oven to 375 F.

Beat eggs well, then add sugar, lemon extract, and anise oil. Beat until thoroughly blended and then add liquid shortening or melted butter and beat for 2 more minutes.

Sift flour and baking powder together and add to the mixture. Beat for 2 minutes until you have a soft dough. If it is too sticky, you can add a little flour.

Shape into 2 flat long rolls and flatten the tops with your fingers. Bake on a greased cookie sheet in preheated for about 25 minutes, or until golden and light brown.

FROSTING

Mix some confection sugar with ½ cup milk, so that you have a very thin glaze. Brush frosting over the cookies with a pastry brush and sprinkle colored candies over the frosting.

Cut logs into cookies when completely cold.

FOR COOKIES WALNUT SIZE

Make long log rolls, cut cookies into 1 inch rounds and bake for 10 minutes.

<Have your children or grandchildren help you. This can be fun Emilia>

Emilia Fusco

BISCOTTI CALABRESI

Calabrian Biscotti

INGREDIENTS

1 pound and 3 oz. all purpose flour

1 envelope dry yeast

3 whole eggs

3½ oz. Crisco

7 oz. sugar

GLAZE

5 oz. confection sugar

3 egg whites

½ the juice of one lemon

DIRECTIONS

Preheat oven to 400 F.

Add flour into a medium bowl. In a small teacup add 3 tablespoons warm water, then add dry yeast and let dissolve for 2 minutes.

To the flour, add yeast, 3 eggs, Crisco and sugar and work dough for 5 minutes until it feels elastic. Cover and put bowl in a warm place for 1 hour.

Sprinkle flour on a wood surface flatten the tough with roll pin to about ½ inch thickness.

Cut cookies into your favorite shapes, grease a baking pan and put cookies

2 inches apart, bake at preheat oven at 400F. for 20 minutes. Let cookies cool off on a wooden surface.

In electric mixer, mix egg whites, lemon juice and confection sugar. Brush the glaze mixture over the cookies.

<Have fun! Emilia>

BISCOTTI CON TATTERI E NOCI

Date & Walnut Cookies

INGREDIENTS

2 eggs

1 cup sugar

2 sticks melted butter or margarine

2 tablespoons milk

8 oz. sour cream

2 teaspoons baking pour

1 teaspoon baking soda

1 teaspoon vanilla

5 cups flour, sifted

1 cup dates, chopped

3 cups walnuts, chopped

FOR THE GLAZE

1 cup confection sugar

2 tablespoons water

DIRECTIONS

Preheat oven to 350 F.

In a large bowl beat eggs and sugar for 1 minute with an electric mixer, then add melted butter, milk and sour cream. Beat until well mixed and then add sour cream, vanilla, baking pour and baking soda. Mix for 2 minutes and then add sifted flour.

Combine thoroughly and then stir in the chopped dates and walnuts.

Sprinkle a wooden surface with flour and work the mixture with your hands for 4 minutes.

Cover a baking pan with parchment paper. Scoop the mixture into balls about the same size as a small meatball and place 2 inches apart from one another. Bake in preheated oven for 15 minutes or until golden brown.

When cookies are cool, mix confection sugar and water, and brush the glaze over the cookies. Let glaze cooling and be form before serve the cookie.

<Enjoy! Emilia>

Emilia Fusco

BISCOTTI ALLE NOCCIOLINE

Hazelnut Biscotti

INGREDIENTS

2 cups all purpose flour

1/3 cup semi-sweet cocoa

1 tablespoon instant espresso powder

1 ½ teaspoon baking pour

1 teaspoon baking soda

¼ teaspoon salt

3 large eggs

½ cup oil extra virgin

1 ½ teaspoon vanilla

1¼ cup hazelnuts, toasted and coarsely chopped

DIRECTIONS

Preheat oven to 375 F.

Sift flour, cocoa, baking powder, espresso powder, baking soda and salt.

Combine 3 eggs and vanilla and mix on low speed for 40 seconds with an electric mixer. Add sugar and beat for 30 seconds, then add oil, and beating well. Add flour 1 cup at time, beating until the mixture is well combine.

Add chopped hazelnuts and mix on low speed. Sprinkle flour on a wooden surface and divide dough into two halves. Roll each piece into a log about 12 inches long.

Transfer the logs to a baking sheet covered with waxed paper, making sure to space them well apart.

Beat 1 egg and brush over the logs to give them a good golden and light color when biscotti are done.

Bake for 30 minutes in preheated oven. Transfer logs to a cutting board and cut into ¾ inch thick slices on the diagonal.

If you prefer biscotti firmer, return to the baking pan after cutting and bake for 5 more minutes.

These biscotti can be stored into plastic container for more then 2 or 3 weeks. Can be also stored into Ziplocs bags and into the freezer. They also make a nice holiday gift for family and friends.

<Enjoy! Emilia>

BISCOTTE AL MIELE E ALLE MANDORLE

Honey & Almond Cookies

INGREDIENTS

1¼ cup honey

½ cup butter

1 egg

2 tablespoons lemon zest

1½ cups flour

2 tablespoons baking powder

1 pinch salt

4 oz. almonds, finely chopped

½ cup almonds, sliced

DIRECTIONS

Preheat oven to 375 F.

With an electric blender beat honey and butter, then add egg and lemon zest. Add flour, baking powder, and salt and mix until thoroughly combined. Add chopped almonds and mix well.

Cover a baking pan with parchment or wax paper. Pour mixture into a cookie bag and use a round point to pipe cookie dough onto the parchment paper, leaving 2½ inches between cookies.

Bake in preheated oven for 15 minutes.

Decorate cookies with sliced almonds and a little powdered sugar.

<Have fun! Emilia>

BISCOTTI DI SAN GIUSEPPE THE CALABRIA

Saint Joseph Cookies From Calabria

INGREDIENTS

2½ cups water

1 stick Crisco

½ teaspoon salt

2 pounds flour, sifted

½ cup confection sugar (sift in with the flour)

1 teaspoon baking powder (sift in with the flour)

2 cups vegetables oil to fry

DIRECTIONS

In a large saucepan add water, Crisco and salt. Put over stove on a low heat.

Add flour, confection sugar and baking powder to the pan a little bit at a time using a colander. Keep stirring until mixture comes to a big boil.

Transfer dough over to a floured surface and dough into logs 12 to 14 inch long and ¾ thick. Cut 3 to 4 inch long.

In a frying pan heat oil until hot, add biscotti and fry until golden.

Transfer biscotti to a dish covered with a paper towel to absorb extra oil.

After about 5 minutes, when biscotti are cool enough, put them onto a serving dish and decorate with powdered sugar.

<Enjoy! Emilia>

BISCOTTI PREFERITI DI PAPA` CON IL VINO BIANCO

My Father's Special Cookies With White Wine

INGREDIENTS

3 cups flour

1 cup white wine

1 egg

¾ cup sugar

1 teaspoon fennel seed

1 pinch of salt

DIRECTIONS

Preheat oven to 400 F.

On a wood surface add flour and make a well in the center. Add all of the remaining ingredients and work with your hands until you have smooth dough.

Roll it out into long log. Cut the long piece, 5 inch long and seal both ands together to make a small cercal.

Dip top side of each cookie into a dish of granulated sugar, and then arrange them on a lightly greased and floured baking pan with the sugar up.

Bake in preheated oven for 20 to 25 minutes. Let cookies cool.

These cookies are well appreciated at parties with a glass of wine.

<Enjoy! And Have fun! Emilia>

TORTA PER IL CAFFE`

Coffee` Cake

INGREDIENTS

½ cup Crisco

1 cup low fat butter milk

½ teaspoon salt

1 teaspoon baking soda

¼ cup chopped walnuts

¾ cup sugar

1 tablespoon confection sugar

DIRECTIONS

In a medium mix bowl, combine buttermilk, Crisco, and sugar, mix on a low speed with electric mix until combine well.

Add salt, baking soda, flour and combine with buttermilk mixture. Grease a 9 inch round sprinkform baking pan.

Bake at 375 F. for 30 to 35 minutes, or until insert to the center a toothpick comes clear. Transfer cake to a wire rack to cool competently.

When cake is cool down, add to the top chopped walnuts, and sprinkle over the confection sugar.

Serve with coffee` or tea.

< Enjoy Emilia>

PARFE` AL LIMONE

Lemon Parfaits

INGREDIENTS

2 cups lemon sherbet softened

1 lemon peel

½ cup Oreo cookies, crumble

10 macadamia nuts finely chopped

4 chilled parfait glass

DIRECTIONS

In a medium bowl combine lemon sherbet and lemon peel. Spoon the lemon mixture into glasses.

Cover first with Oreo cookies, then with chopped macadamia nuts.

Chill into freezer for 10 minutes before serving.

<Enjoy Emilia>

ITALIA COFFE` AL GHIACCIO

Ice Italian Coffee`

INGREDIENTS

6 teaspoon instant espresso coffee`

1 ox coffee` brand

6 teaspoons sugar

1 ½ cup boiling water

6 teaspoon chocolate syrup

Ice cubes

DIRECTIONS

In a bowl dissolve coffee` with hot water. Add sugar, milk, and chocolate syrups.

Stir well until combine mixture together.

Serve over Ice cubes. Makes 3 servings.

<This is for adult only>

<Have fun Emilia>

MOUSSE DI CHIOCCOLATO BIANCO

White Chocolate Mousse

INGREDIENTS

1 package frozen Pastry dough

6 squares I oz each white chocolate

1 ½ cups have cream

1 square semi sweet chocolate, melted

DIRECTIONS

Bake and cool pastry dough, according to package direction. In microwave safe bowl add white chocolate and ¼ cup cream, on high speed for two minutes melted the chocolate, stirring halfway through heating.

Stir until chocolate is completely melted. Cool for 20 minutes or until room temperature, stir occasional. In a chili bowl place remaining cream.

Beat with electric mixture at medium speed until soft picks form. Do not overheat.

Fold half the whipped cream into chocolate mixture.

Fold reaming whipped cream just until blend. Spoon into pastry shells. Drizzle with melted chocolate. Refrigerate for 1 hour.

Makes 6 pastries.

<Indulge your self with small portion. Emilia>

BUDINO ALLE PESCHE

Peach Pudding

INGREDIENTS

12 vanilla waffles

5 tablespoons sugar

1 tablespoon corn starch

¼ teaspoon salt

1 cup peaches peel and thinly slice

2 eggs yolk

1 ½ cup milk

DIRECTIONS

Over a double boiler combine sugar, cornstarch, and salt. Gradually add milk and eggs yolk. Stirring continually until mixture blended together.

Place over simmering water, continually stirring, cook for 5 t0 6 minutes or until mixture is thick and smooth. Remove from heat, stirring in slice peaches.

Divide mixture equal into 4 custard or budding dish. Arrange 3 vanilla waffles around the edge dish.

Cover with cling wrap and chill for 2 to 3 hours before serving.

<Indulge your self! Emilia>

PARFE` AL CAPPUCCINO

Cappuccino Parfaits

INGREDIENTS

3 cups vanilla ice scream

1 tablespoon instant espresso coffee

4 tablespoon coffee brand

4 tablespoons whipped cream for topping

½ cup chocolate waffles crumbs

8 mint leaves

DIRECTIONS

In a small bowl combine ice scream and espresso instant coffee, and stirring well to blend evenly. Spoon ice scream mixture into 4 equally parfaits glass.

Top ice scream with 1 tablespoon coffee brand, then 1 tablespoon crumbs waffles.

Repeat layers with the ice scream, crumbs waffles.

Top each glass with 1 tablespoon whipped cream. Cover each glass with wrap peppers. Freeze for 1 to 1 ½ hours before serving.

Before serving garnish each parfaits with 2 mint leaves and 1 espresso coffee beans.

<Enjoy Emilia>

SCIRUPPO DI ARANCE SANGUIGNE

Blood Orange Syrup

INGREDIENTS

3 cups freshly squeezed blood orange juice

3 tablespoons Crystals cane sugar

1 teaspoon vanilla extract

1 bay leaf

4 thin slice peeled ginger

¼ teaspoon salt

DIRECTIONS

Combine all ingredients in a small, and heavy saucepan. Bring to a boil and cook uncovered until the sauce is reduce by half.

Remove bay leaves and ginger. Cool to room temperature.

Serve over your favorite ice scream or desserts.

<Enjoy Emilia>

SHIRUPPO ALLE FRAGOLE

Strawberry Syrup

INGREDIENTS

6 cups fresh strawberry, quarterly slice

½ cup sugar

2 tablespoons lemon juice

1 tablespoon lemon zest

2/3 cup strawberry juice

DIRECTIONS

In a heavy saucepan combine 3 cups strawberry, sugar and juice. Simmer over medium heat and stirring often for 5 to 8 minutes.

Add remaining strawberry, lemon zest and lemon juice.

Continue stirring and simmer over low medium heat for 3 to 5 minutes or until syrup coat a spoon.

Serve warm, or cool over your favorite ice scream, piece of cake or over a waffle.

<Indulge your self. Emilia>

MIA MAMMA FICHI SECCHI IMBOTTITI

My Mother Stuffed Dried Figs

INGREDIENTS

24 dried figs

24 half walnuts

1 tablespoon cinnamon

¼ cup granulated sugar

DIRECTIONS

Open dried figs in half star from the top, when get to the bottom stop cut.

Open figs and in each fig put half the walnuts: close and with your fingers press figs together.

In a cookie baking pan with line of parchment paper, bake figs at preheat oven at 375 F. for 5 to 8 minutes, or until figs are golden and light brown.

Transfer figs on a cooling rack. In a plastic bag, add sugar and cinnamon, shake to mix well.

Add figs and shake the bag to coat well figs with sugar mixture.

Preserved in a plastic contain, or in a wooden boxes, line with oven paper.

<Enjoy Emilia>

MIA MAMMA CILIEGIE SOTTO L`ALCOLO

My Mother Cherries & Alcohol

INGREDIENTS

2 pounds cherries

½ cup sugar

1 bottle or 4 cups pure alcohol (95 C.)

2 sticks cinnamon

DIRECTIONS

When by the cherrieschoose them one by one: they need to be very hard and clear.

Cut the stem about 1 inch long. Wash cherries with cool water, and let dried over paper towel.

In a Mason jar add cherries, sugar and cinnamon sticks. Add alcohol and cover, leave ½ inch down from the top.

Seal jar and put in the cool place in the house. After a week open jars and see if they need more alcohol and add little more.

Cherries needed to be in the alcohol about 2 months before being eaten.

<Use these methods to make: grapes with the alcohol, Emilia>

TORTA ALLE NOCI

Walnut Cake

INGREDIENTS

2 cups all purpose flour

2 eggs

½ cup soften butter

¾ cup sugar

¾ cup milk

2 tablespoons baking soda

1 teaspoon vanilla extract

¾ cup small chopped walnuts

1 tablespoon orange zest

¼ teaspoon salt

DIRECTIONS

In a large mix bowl add soft butter and sugar. Mix on low speed to combine well sugar and butter. Add eggs one at a time and keep beating after each egg.

Add orange zest to the mixture. Sift flour, baking soda, baking pour, and salt.

Gradually add flour to the butter mixture one cup at a time. Aft the first cup flour add milk and beat at low speed: then add the last cup flour.

Grease and flour a round spring form cake pan. Bake at preheat oven at 375 F. for 25 to 30 minutes or until toothpick comes clear from the center of the cake.

Cool cake 5 minutes before remove from the pan. Cool over wire rack.

Serve plain or with your favorite frosting.

<Have fun Emilia>

VARIAZIONE PER DECORARE LE TORTE

Variety of Toppings For Cakes

INGREDIENTS

1 cup powdered sugar

2 tablespoons water

½ tablespoon lemon extract

DIRECTIONS

In a bowl mix all 3 ingredients until soften and creamed. With wood spatula spread over the cake.

INGREDIENTS

1 cup powdered sugar

1 tablespoon cinnamon

2 tablespoon water

1 tablespoon lemon juice

DIRECTIONS

The same directions as above.

INGREDIENTS

1 pkg. 8 oz cream cheese softened

1 pound powdered sugar

1 stick soften margarine

¼ tablespoon almonds shave for topping decoration

DIRECTIONS

The same directions about. Decorate frosting with shave almonds.

Regarding all type of frosting. Emphasize your taste. You can add 1 tablespoon brown sugar, powdered sugar. Add 2 tablespoon semisweet cocoa powdered and you have chocolate frosting.

I wrote this book with passion to remember my beautiful Mother. I enjoy very much. I hope you will enjoy it in the kitchen.

<Good luck on this adventure. Emilia>

INDEX

ABOUT THE AUTHOR

Emilia was born and raised in Calabria, Italy. She came to this country at the age of 26. Emilia married her husband, Peter also from Italy at the age of 28. They have two children, Alberto and Silvia and 3 beautiful grandchildren.

As a young girl she enjoyed cooking with her mother and has now passed the same love to her family. Her recipes have been in her family for many years. Now she is sharing with you her own special taste of Calabria.

Printed in the United States
203459BV00005BB/2/A